OXFORD
UNIVERSITY PRESS

Norman Whitney

Student Book

3

CONTENTS

Let's remember!

	Unit 1	**Unit 3**	**Unit 5**
Presentation	New York, New York!	An American deli.	On Broadway!
Communication & Pronunciation	Possession: *whose?* Offers and replies The sounds /a/, /ə/ and /ɔ/	Preferences Apologies The sounds /æ/, /e/ and /ɔ/	Obligation (*have to*) and prohibition (*can't*) Obligation (*have to*) and lack of obligation (*don't have to*) Final consonants /ŋ/ and /ŋk/; /s/ and /z/
Grammar & Study skills	Simple past. Present perfect Simple past and present perfect Relative pronouns *who* and *which/that* Relative pronoun *whose*	Present perfect with *for* and *since* Present perfect with *just, already, yet* Adverbs of manner Are you a good language learner?	Zero conditional First conditional *need*, *have to* and *can't*

	Unit 2	**Unit 4**	**Unit 6**
Presentation & Culture	My kind of town.	Famous Americans.	Welcome to Oz!
Vocabulary	American English and British English	Feelings and emotions	Word formation: prefixes
Writing	Building sentences: Writing about places	Building paragraphs: Writing about movies and books	Planning and making notes: Writing about vacations
Song & Progress review	Good Thing Progress review units 1 & 2	What Have I Done to Deserve This? Progress review units 3 & 4	On Broadway Progress review units 5 & 6

Review UNITS 1 to 4

Bonus units
1. An American tradition: Thanksgiving (p.66)
2. A British tradition: Wimbledon (p.68)
3. Festivals, celebrations, customs, and traditions! (p.70)

Communication activities (p.72)

Unit 7	Unit 9	Unit 11	
Champions.	In-line skating in the park.	Graduation day.	Presentation
gical deductions: *must be, can't be* equence: *first … then … finally …* The sounds /ɪ/ /e/ and /ʊ/	Good news, bad news! Reporting opinions Stress and rhythm	Well-wishing *Thanks!* Intonation	Communication & Pronunciation
Passive Passive with *by* + agent gical deductions: *must be, can't be* How do you practice English?	Reported speech: with reporting verbs in the present Reported speech: with reporting verbs in the past Indefinite pronouns	Second conditional Possessive pronouns How do you study for tests?	Grammar & Study skills
Unit 8	**Unit 10**	**Unit 12**	
The secret of life.	The world of sports.	Varieties of English.	Presentation & Culture
Word formation: suffixes	New sports! Dangerous sports!	Word families	Vocabulary
Expanding plans and notes: Writing about jobs	Connecting ideas: Writing about special people	Sequencing events: Writing about special occasions	Writing
When Will I be Loved? Progress review 7 & 8	Sisters are Doin' it for Themselves Progress review units 9 & 10	Money, Money, Money! Progress review units 11 & 12	Song & Progress review

Review UNITS 5 to 8   **Review** UNITS 9 to 12

Stories
Number One (p.78)
Mountain Mystery (p.81)

Grammar help (p.84)
Word list (p.92)
Word formation: prefixes and suffixes (p.95)

Let's remember.

Grammar

Irregular verbs: simple past

> **REMEMBER!**
>
> We use the simple past to talk about actions completed at a specific time in the past.
>
> I **went** to the rock concert last night.
> She **didn't go** to the rock concert last night.
> **Did** you **go** to the rock concert last night?
> Yes I **did**./No I **didn't**.

1 Match the base forms of the irregular verbs with their simple past forms.

1 build – built

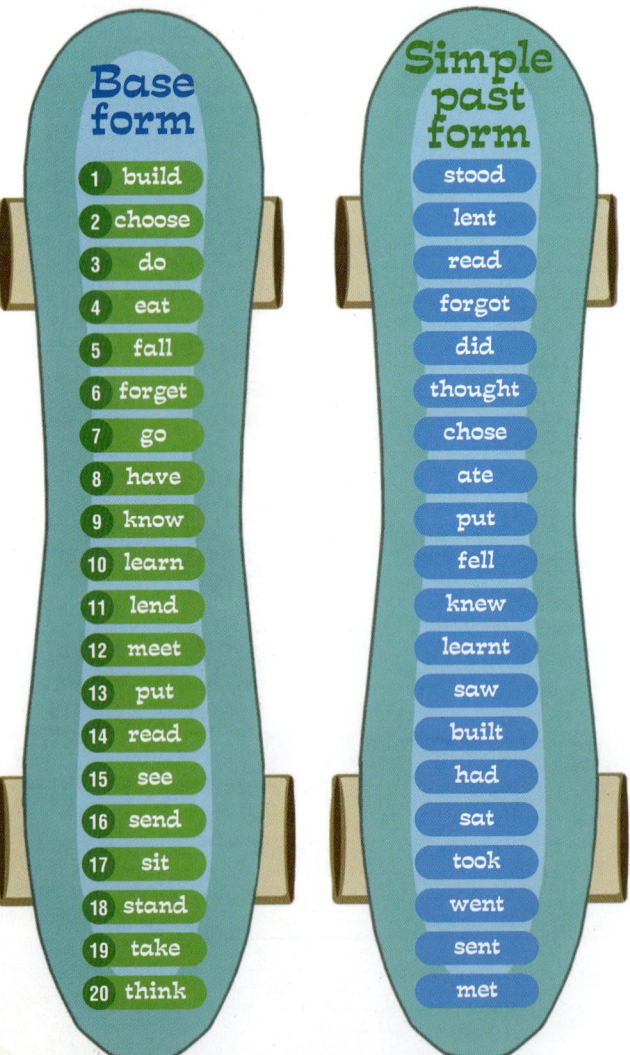

Base form
1. build
2. choose
3. do
4. eat
5. fall
6. forget
7. go
8. have
9. know
10. learn
11. lend
12. meet
13. put
14. read
15. see
16. send
17. sit
18. stand
19. take
20. think

Simple past form
- stood
- lent
- read
- forgot
- did
- thought
- chose
- ate
- put
- fell
- knew
- learnt
- saw
- built
- had
- sat
- took
- went
- sent
- met

2 Read about Marco's vacation in the USA. Change the verbs (1–10) into the simple past (affirmative and negative).

Last winter, my friend Alex and I (**go**) went to the USA on vacation with a group from our college. It was our first vacation without our parents, and we (**1 have**) a fantastic time! We (**2 choose**) to go to Aspen, Colorado because I love snowboarding. Alex (**3 not know**) how to snowboard, but he (**4 learn**) on our first day there.

At our hotel we (**5 meet**) a Polish couple called Jan and Zofia. They were very generous. Zofia (**6 lend**) me her digital camera. I (**7 take**) some photos and (**8 send**) them to our friends and family in Brazil. The best photo is of Alex, when he (**9 fall**) off his snowboard. He (**10 not think**) it was funny, but I did!

3 Rearrange the words and phrases to make questions about Exercise 2. Then, answer the questions.

enjoy / their vacation? / Did / Marco and Alex

Q Did Marco and Alex enjoy their vacation?
A Yes, they did.

1 parents / Marco's / with them? / go / Did
2 in Aspen? / learn / Alex / Did / how to snowboard
3 lend / Did / her digital camera? / Zofia / Marco
4 laugh / Alex / when / Did / he fell off / his snowboard?

Past continuous

4 First, study the Remember! box. Then, complete the rule below.

REMEMBER!

We use the *past continuous* to talk about continuous actions at a specific time in the past.

I **was watching** TV at eight o'clock last night.

He **was not / wasn't watching** TV at eight o'clock last night.

Were you **watching** TV at eight o'clock last night?

Yes, I **was**. / No, I **wasn't**.

 The past continuous = _____ /were + verb + ing.

5 Study the picture. Write four affirmative and four negative sentences about what the people at the music festival were doing or not doing at three o'clock.

At three o'clock …
Milo *was making* lunch.
The 3-Tones *weren't sleeping*.

6 Look at the picture in exercise 5 again. Complete the questions with *was* or *were*. Then, answer the questions.

Q *Was* Milo making lunch?
A Yes, he *was*.

1 ____ Yugi and Teri shopping?
2 ____ The 3-Tones playing on stage?
3 ____ Milo laughing?
4 ____ Saskia talking on her phone?
5 ____ Milo's dog sleeping?

Simple past with *ago*

7 Rewrite the sentences using *ago*.

David left the house at one o'clock.
It is now three o'clock.
David left the house two hours ago.

1 I ate breakfast at eight o'clock.
  It is now eleven o'clock.
2 Mary met her boyfriend in January.
  It is now June.
3 They built this house in 1940.
  It is now 2004.
4 We saw that movie on Monday.
  It is now Friday.

Simple past and past continuous

8 Complete the story. Use the simple past (six verbs) and the past continuous (six verbs). Then, listen and check your answers.

I (shop) *was shopping* in town last Saturday when I (start) *started* to feel hungry. So I (**1 go**) into a fast food restaurant and ordered a soda and an apple pie. The place was very busy, so I (**2 sit**) down next to a good-looking guy. He (**3 read**) a motorcycle magazine.

While I (**4 sit**) there with my soda, I noticed the guy suddenly pick up my apple pie and take a bite! Then, while I (**5 try**) to think of something to say to him, he (**6 do**) it again! So I (**7 stand**) up and started shouting at him. I was really angry.

While I (**8 shout**) at this guy, a waitress arrived at our table. She (**9 carry**) my apple pie on a tray! "You (**10 forget**) this, Madam …" she said. I was so embarrassed! Luckily, the guy (**11 think**) it was funny, and we both laughed. And we laughed about it again the next day, while we (**12 have**) dinner together!

Grammar

Comparative and superlative adjectives

1 Complete the chart.

Base form	Comparative	Superlative
tall	taller	the tallest
(1) warm	_____	the warmest
(2) nice	nicer	_____
(3) _____	gentler	the gentlest
(4) easy	_____	the easiest
(5) heavy	heavier	_____
(6) _____	worse	the worst
(7) good	_____	_____
(8) _____	farther	_____
(9) _____	more intelligent	the most intelligent
(10) important	_____	_____

REMEMBER!

We use *comparatives* to compare two people, places, or things.

We use *superlatives* to compare three or more people, places, or things.

2 First, look at the pictures and study the information. Then, write affirmative comparisons. Use a comparative adjective and *than*.

Name	Alan	Anita	Nelson
Age	16	17	18
Shoe size	11	5	8
100m in seconds	16.5	16.8	15.5

Alan is (**tall**) Anita.
Alan is taller than Anita.

1 Anita is (**old**) Alan.
2 Nelson's feet are (**big**) Anita's.
3 Alan is (**fast**) Anita.
4 Alan's hair is (**long**) Nelson's.

3 Look at the pictures and information in exercise 2 again. Write negative comparisons. Use *not as ... as*.
Anita is not as tall as Alan.

4 Look at the pictures and information in exercise 2 again. Complete the sentences with the comparative and superlative forms of the adjectives in parentheses.
Anita is older than Alan, but Nelson is the oldest. (**old**)

1 Anita is _____ Nelson, but Alan is _____ (**young**).
2 Nelson's feet are _____ Alan's, but Anita's are _____ (**small**).
3 Alan is _____ than Nelson, but Anita is _____ (**slow**).
4 Nelson's feet are _____ Anita's, but Alan's are _____ (**big**).

5 First, make the questions, using the superlative form. Then, ask and answer with a partner.

Which are (**big**) animals in the world?
Q Which are *the biggest* animals in the world?
A Whales

1 Which is (**long**) river in the world?
2 Where is (**cold**) place on Earth?
3 Which is (**near**) planet to the Sun?
4 Who is (**tall**) person in the class?
5 Who has (**short**) hair in the class?

will and *going to*

REMEMBER!

We use *will* for
a) predictions about the future,
One day, you will be a very rich person.
b) instant decisions,
Would you like a drink? Yes, I'll have a glass of orange juice please.
c) offers of help.
Your bags look heavy. We'll carry them for you.

We use *going to* for
d) plans and intentions,
I'm going to study computing at college.
e) predictions about things you can see or hear.
Look! He's going to score!

6 **Match the sentences (1–5) with the meanings (a–e) in the Remember! box.**

   Soon we will do all of our shopping on the Internet.   a
   1 Q: Can I help you? A: Yes, I'll have a cheese sandwich, please. ___
   2 Mark is going to be a police officer when he graduates. ___
   3 Be careful! You're going to break those glasses. ___
   4 Are you cold? I'll turn on the heat. ___
   5 You will not find a cheaper car than this! ___

7 **Complete the sentences using *will* or *(be) going to*.**

   They (**not stop**). They *aren't going to stop.*
   1 They (**crash**)!

   2 We (**see**) a rock concert.
   3 I (**come**) with you.

   4 In the future, children (**not go**) to school for classes.
   5 I (**help**) you with that.

Present perfect (affirmative and negative)

> **REMEMBER!**
>
> We use the present perfect to:
> a) talk about experiences,
>   *I have been* to Japan.
>   *We've never met* before.
> b) connect the past with the present.
>   Look! *She's made* a wonderful meal for us! Let's eat!
>   *I haven't eaten* today.

8 **Complete the sentences using the present perfect of the verbs in parentheses.**

   I (**not tell**) Dad that I (**borrow**) his car!
   I *haven't told* Dad that *I've borrowed* his car.

   1 I (**read**) the book, but I (**not see**) the movie.
   2 She (**know**) him all her life, and they (**never argue**).
   3 I (**make**) a delicious meal and you (**not touch**) it! Are you sick?
   4 He (**never study**) in his life, but he (**pass**) all his tests!
   5 They (**build**) a new sports center in town, but we (**not go**) there.

Present perfect (question forms) with *ever*

9 **Ask and answer with a partner.**

   Have you ever seen a kangaroo?   —   No, never!

   Have you ever …

   Has your mom/sister/friend ever …

   … been to the USA?   —   Yes, I have.

   … eaten Japanese food?   —   No, I haven't.

   … studied Russian?   —   Yes, she has.

   … played in a band?   —   No, she hasn't.

   You choose!

Vocabulary

Transportation

1 Complete the story with kinds of transportation. Then, listen and check your answers.

AN EXCITING TRIP

When Mike graduated at 18 he decided to go on a trip around the world before he went to college. The first part of his trip was by **t**rain from Manchester to Liverpool. There he bought a one-way ticket to go by **(1) s**___ to New York. It was a long slow journey, and he wanted a faster kind of transportation to cross America, so he bought a **(2) m**___ . Unfortunately, he crashed it in the desert in Colorado. Fortunately, a kind driver gave him a ride in his **(3) t**___ all the way to California. Mike stayed for three days in San Francisco then got a **(4) p**___ to Australia. He bought a **(5) v**___ in Sydney and drove all the way across Australia in two weeks. Then he flew to Asia. He was starting to run out of money now, so he traveled from East Asia to Europe mostly by **(6) b**___ and on **(7) f**___ He crossed Poland in two days, and finally reached France on his nineteenth birthday, when he got on a **(8) b**___ to take him back to England. Unfortunately there was a storm and he fell into the ocean. He was in the ocean for two hours before a **(9) h**___ picked him up and took him to a hospital in London. He was OK, but what a trip! Now Mike travels everywhere by **(10) b**___ and he never goes very far from home!

Towns and buildings

2 Match the pictures (1–9) with the words in the box.

> church   movie theater   bank
> book store   bus station   museum
> park   post office   grocery store

1 church

8

At the restaurant

3 Complete the restaurant review. Change the pictures into words.

RESTAURANT PORCINI

REVIEW BY MAX TYLER

STAR RATING: ★

Restaurant Porcini has just opened on Fifth Avenue, so my partner and I decided to try it. What a big mistake! When we arrived, the waiter was reading the newspaper. We waited for five minutes before he showed us to our table! When we sat down, we saw that the **(1)**  had a big hole in it, my partner's **(2)** was dirty, and my **(3)** was broken.

We ordered our appetizers. My partner's **(4)** was OK, but when my **(5)** arrived, the waiter had his thumb in it. When I told him this he said, "Don't worry, sir. The soup isn't very hot," and cleaned his thumb on my **(6)** ! I couldn't eat the soup even if I wanted to because he forgot to bring me a **(7)** 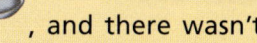, and there wasn't any **(8)** . We didn't stay for our main courses. I've never been to a worse restaurant.

Take my advice: don't go there!

Describing people: personality

4 Match the personality adjectives (1–7) with their opposites (a–g).

1 generous – b cheap

1 generous	a) shy
2 hard-working	b) cheap
3 polite	c) lazy
4 confident	d) rude
5 cheerful	e) impatient
6 modest	f) vain
7 patient	g) sad

5 Complete the sentences. Use words from exercise 4.

She studies a lot and has a job on the weekends. She's very hard-working.

1 He always tells people how wonderful he is, and loves looking in the mirror. He's _____ .
2 She hates waiting. She's _____ .
3 He laughs a lot and is always happy. He's _____ .
4 She is very smart and successful, but she doesn't talk about it. She's _____ .
5 He doesn't have much money, but he gives a lot to other people. He's very _____ .

Personal computers

6 First, read the advert below. Then, label the picture with the words in bold.

FOR SALE:

One PC, 750Mhz, 64Mb RAM, 10Gb hard drive, 600mm **monitor**. It takes CDs, **DVD**s, and **floppy disks**. Includes **keyboard, mouse, modem** and **speakers** – $300 for everything. **Color printer** also for sale – $100, or $50 with the computer. Free **mouse pad** included if I like you ☺.

Contact Julie – 555-1212.

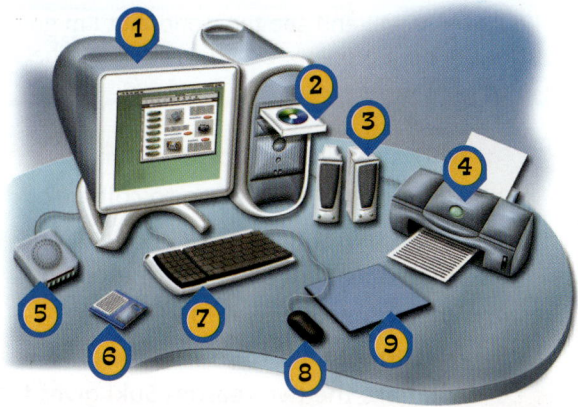

WORD LIST   page 92

Skills work — Life after school

Reading

1 Suki and James both graduate next summer. Read about their plans and hopes. Then, answer the questions.

LIFE AFTER SCHOOL — Suki

My favorite subjects at school are English and Spanish, and I'd like to continue learning languages when I graduate next summer. But I don't want to go straight to college. I want to travel first. I've never left Japan before, and I'd love to go to the USA for a few months. We see so much about the USA on TV and at the movies, I'd like to go and see what it's really like! It will be great practice for my English, too.

When I get back from my travels I'll go to college in Tokyo and study English and Spanish. I'm going to be a teacher – but not here in Japan. I'd like to live in the USA and teach Japanese!

LIFE AFTER SCHOOL — James

I'm studying economics and history at school here in Boston right now. Most of my friends are going to go to college next year, but I don't want to. I don't really enjoy studying. I'd like to get a job as soon as I can because I want to make some money. I'm going to save up my money and start my own business. I haven't decided what the business will be exactly, but it will probably involve computers and the Internet. I'm always surfing the Net!

I'd like to travel and see the world, but I'm going to wait until I can afford to do it properly. One day, I'd like to be very rich!

    Who is studying history?   **James**
1. Who doesn't want to go to college?
2. Who is going to go traveling first, Suki or James?
3. Who wants to make a lot of money?
4. Where does Suki want to live?
5. Why does James want to get a job?
6. What are the two reasons Suki gives for wanting to visit the USA?

Listening

2 Listen to the interview with Natasha. Choose the correct answers.

Natasha is studying math, physics and,
- a biology.
- (b) chemistry.
- c geography.

1. What is Natasha going to do when she graduates?
   - a go on vacation
   - b study
   - c work
2. Where is Natasha's summer job?
   - a in a restaurant
   - b in a bank
   - c in a coffee shop
3. What is Natasha going to buy with her money from the summer job?
   - a a computer
   - b sound equipment
   - c clothes
4. What is Natasha going to study at college?
   - a music
   - b dancing
   - c computer science

Speaking

3 Ask and answer with a partner.

- What do you want to do after graduation?
- I'd like to travel
- I'm going to get a job.
- I'm going to go straight to college.
- I don't want to study.
- I'd love to go to the USA.
- I want to take a year out.

You choose!

Writing

4 Write a short text entitled *Life after school*. Use the examples in exercise 1 to help you.

Writing Guide

What are you doing now?
Right now, I'm _____.
What would you like to do when you graduate? Why?
After graduation, I'd like to _____.
What don't you want to do? Why?
I don't want to _____ because _____.
What would you like to do in the future?
In the future, I'd like to _____.

Song — Dancin' in the Street

1 Listen and complete the song. Use the words in the box.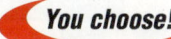

> Chicago   here   there   everywhere
> New Orleans   ~~world~~   everywhere
> New York City   world

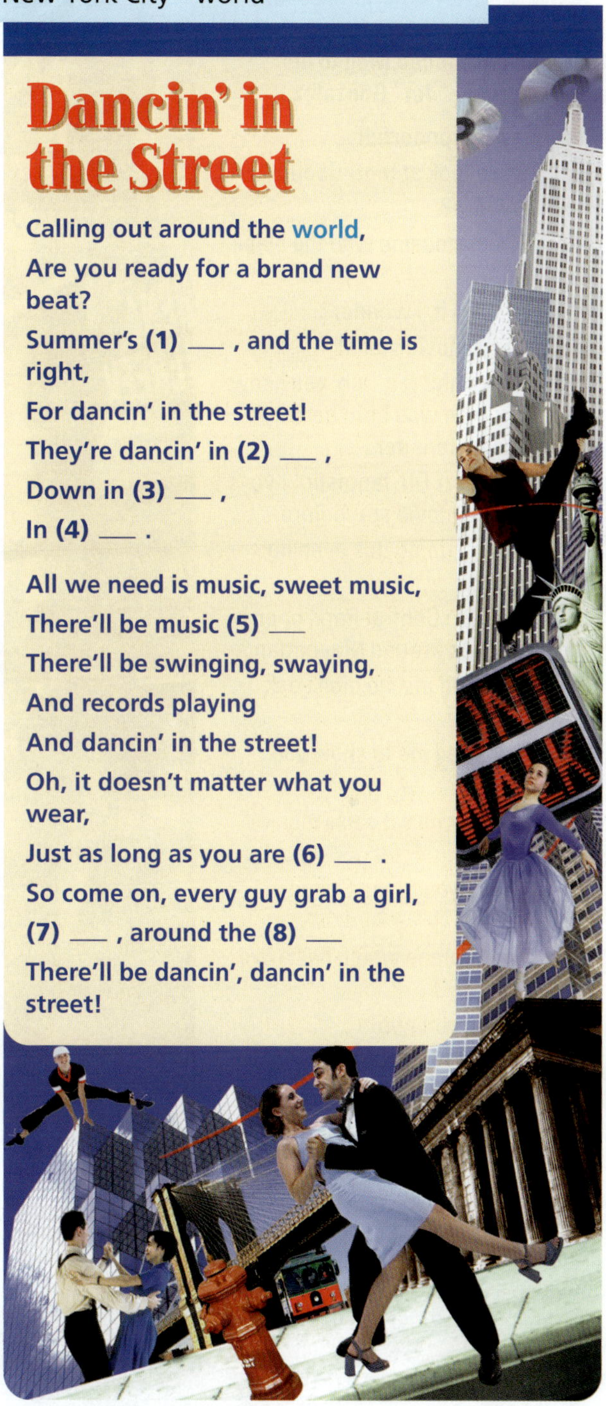

Dancin' in the Street

Calling out around the world,
Are you ready for a brand new beat?
Summer's (1) ___ , and the time is right,
For dancin' in the street!
They're dancin' in (2) ___ ,
Down in (3) ___ ,
In (4) ___ .

All we need is music, sweet music,
There'll be music (5) ___
There'll be swinging, swaying,
And records playing
And dancin' in the street!
Oh, it doesn't matter what you wear,
Just as long as you are (6) ___ .
So come on, every guy grab a girl,
(7) ___ , around the (8) ___
There'll be dancin', dancin' in the street!

2 How many American cities are there in the song? Where are they in the USA?

3 Can you think of any other songs about celebrations or parties? In your opinion, are they better than *Dancin' in the Street*? What is your favorite party song?

1 New York, New York!

Meg O'Connor comes from London. Two weeks ago, she flew to New York. She is going to live with her American cousin Tom Sikora and his parents for a year. This morning, Tom introduced Meg to his classmate, Antonio "Jet" Gonzalez.

Meg New York is wonderful!
Jet Man, take a look at that! Cool!
Tom What? Where?
Jet There! The limousine with the black windows.
Meg Whose limo is it, I wonder?
Tom Maybe it's a movie star's!
Jet Yes! You're right! It's – oh, you know, the singer who was born here in New York … Jennifer …
Meg Jennifer Lopez! Oh, fantastic! I've never seen a movie star before.
Jet What are you doing this evening, Meg?
Tom We're going to Central Park, or on a boat that goes around Manhattan.
Meg Tom! Jet asked *me*, he didn't ask you!
Tom But you wanted me to show you New York.
Jet Have you ever heard salsa music, Meg?
Tom Or I can take you to the Statue of Liberty.
Jet But I know a place which has a live salsa band, and …
Meg Stop fighting you two!

Later …

Jet Would you like to eat, Meg?
Meg No thanks, Jet.
Jet Or would you like a drink? It's on me!
Meg Yes, please. I would.
Tom Yeah, thanks for the offer, Jet. I'll have an extra large juice!
Jet Oh, but – Oh, OK! I'll pay for you, too.

Comprehension

1 Complete the sentences with the correct names. Choose from *Meg, Tom, Jet*.

Meg is from England.
1 ___ and ___ are cousins.
2 ___ and ___ are classmates.
3 ___ is the first person to see the limousine.
4 ___ offers to buy ___ a drink.

What's your opinion?
Why are Tom and Jet fighting?

2 Who says these expressions?

You're right! Jet
1 Stop fighting! _____
2 It's on me! _____
3 Thanks for the offer. _____

How do you say these expressions in your language?

Communication

Possession: *whose*?

3 Listen and repeat. Then, ask and answer with a partner.

Boy Whose jacket is this?
Girl It's John's.
Boy Whose are these sneakers?
Girl They're my brother's.

baseball cap / Maria's
gloves / my dad's
magazines / our cousins'
scarf / my sister's

You choose!

Offers and replies

4 Listen and repeat. Then, practice with a partner. Use the Communication box to help you.

Girl Would you like a coffee?
Boy Yes, please, I would.
Girl Can I buy you an ice-cream cone?
Boy No, thanks. I'm fine.
Girl Can I get you some cake?
Boy Thanks. Yes.

Communication		
How to offer	How to reply "Yes!"	How to reply "No"
Would you like a …?	Yes, please, I would.	No, thanks. I wouldn't.
Can I buy you an …?	Thanks. Yes.	No, thanks. I'm fine.
Can I get you some …?	Sure! Thanks.	No. I'm OK thanks.

Pronunciation

The sounds /a/, /ə/ and /ɔ/

5 Listen and repeat.

/a/	/ə/	/ɔ/
star	bird	walk
arm	word	claw
father	turning	law

The sounds of poetry

6 Listen and repeat. Practice reading the poem aloud.

A bird came down the walk
He did not know I saw;
He bit an angle-worm in halves
And ate the fellow, raw.

Emily Dickinson (1830–1886)

1

Grammar

Simple past

1 Complete the paragraphs. Use the simple past.

Simon works for a successful recording company. Three days ago, he **(visit)** visited his old high school, to talk about his job.

He **(1 take)** some CDs with him, and **(2 play)** them for the students. One girl **(3 ask)**, "**(4 you do)** any of the songs on those CDs?" "Yes," said Simon. "I **(5 be)** the sound engineer on all the tracks."

The students **(6 enjoy)** Simon's talk. He **(7 tell)** them, "When I **(8 attend)** this school a few years ago, I **(9 not study)** very hard. So I **(10 not pass)** many tests." Then he **(11 add)**, "It's different now. Engineers in the music industry need qualifications."

At the end of his talk, he **(12 give)** each student a free CD!

Present perfect

2 Complete the conversation. Use the present perfect.

Boy   **(you ever meet)** Have you ever met Madonna?

Simon   **(1 I ever meet)** Madonna? Yes, **(2 I see)** her a lot. She's great.

Girl   **(3 your company ever make)** a record with *Maroon 5*?

Simon   No. **(4 we not record)** them. **(5 I go)** to one of their concerts. But **(6 I never like)** them!

Simple past and present perfect

3 Study the sentences (a–d), and answer the questions (1–4).

a) Simon **started** his job two years ago.
b) Simon **has never worked** with *Maroon 5*.
c) Simon and his friend **have been to** New York.
d) Simon and his friend **saw** a movie last night.

1 Which two sentences are in the **simple past**?
2 Which two sentences are in the **present perfect**?
3 Which two sentences refer to **a specific time in the past**?
4 Which two sentences **talk about experiences or connect the past to the present**?

4 Complete the sentences. In each pair, use the simple past in one sentence, and the present perfect in the other.

a) I **(buy)** bought a Madonna CD this morning.
b) I **(play)** 've played it three times this evening!

1 a) Simon's brother **(never visit)** New York.
  b) But their parents **(go)** to New York ten years ago.
2 a) I **(not hear)** his new single. What's it like?
  b) Terrible! I **(not like)** it at all.
3 a) You **(see)** *MTV* last night?
  b) No. We **(not watch)** it for a long time.
4 a) We **(go)** to Las Vegas last weekend.
  b) You're lucky! I **(never go)** there.

Relative pronouns *who* and *which / that*

5 First, compare the a) and b) sentences.
1. a) An engineer is a person.
   He or she makes things.
   b) An engineer is a person **who** makes things.
2. a) Dinosaurs were animals.
   They lived millions of years ago.
   b) Dinosaurs were animals **which/that** lived millions of years ago.
3. a) A DVD player is a machine.
   It shows movies.
   b) A DVD player is a machine **which/that** shows movies.

6 Now complete the rule. Use *who*, or *which / that*.

1. We use the relative pronoun ___ for people.
2. We use the relative pronoun ___ or ___ for animals and things.

7 Combine each pair of sentences to make definitions. Use *who* or *which / that*.

Robots are machines.
They can build cars.

Robots are machines *which* can build cars.

1. A clown is a person.
   He/she works in a circus.
2. Microsoft is a company.
   It makes computer software.
3. Aspirin is a medicine.
   It cures headaches.
4. Pilots are people.
   They fly planes.
5. Snakes are reptiles.
   They don't have legs.

8 Work in small groups. Write definitions for these words.

A chef is a person who cooks food.

A lawnmower is a machine that cuts grass.

People	Machines
a chef	a lawnmower
a farmer	a refrigerator
a nurse	a vacuum cleaner
a store clerk	a video recorder
a teacher	a washing machine

Relative pronoun *whose*

9 Study the example. Then, combine the sentences using *whose*.

Mel Gibson is a movie star. His most successful movie is *Braveheart*.

Mel Gibson is a movie star *whose* most successful movie is *Braveheart*.

1. Gloria Estefan is a superstar. Her hits include *Conga!* and *Another*.
2. Venus Williams is a tennis player. Her first major success was at Wimbledon in 2000.
3. Shakespeare was a writer. His plays include *Hamlet* and *Macbeth*.

GRAMMAR HELP! pages 84–85

2 My kind of town.

Reading

1 Read the text. Match the titles (A–E) with the paragraphs (1–5). Then, listen and check your answers.

A A musical mix
B The friendly city
C For the sports fan
D Something for everyone
E Fine dining

1 _B The friendly city_

"Chicago is… my kind of town!" sang Frank Sinatra back in the 1960s. Today, most people who have been to this northern US city feel the same way. With its population of nearly 3 million, and its reputation for friendliness, Chicago inspires the affection of everyone who knows it.

2 _____

Since its first resident, Jean Baptiste Point du Sable, settled there in 1779 Chicago has attracted immigrants from all over the world. They brought their cooking styles with them, making the city a food-lover's paradise. Chicagoans are famous for being enthusiastic meat eaters. They are very proud of the fact that in their city you will find the best hamburgers and hot dogs in the world!

3 _____

Music plays a big part in Chicago's cultural life. Blues and jazz musicians have flocked there since 1915, so it is a great place to hear live music. Every summer, Grant Park hosts the three-day long Chicago Blues Festival, the Chicago Gospel Festival, and the Chicago Jazz Festival. For those with more classical tastes, there is always the Chicago Symphony Orchestra.

4 _____

True Chicagoans love their sports. The city is home to football's _Bears_, ice hockey's _Blackhawks_, basketball's _Bulls_, and baseball's _Cubs_. Wrigley Field is one of the oldest stadiums in the USA, and the Chicago _Cubs_ have played there since 1914. The "Cubbies" don't win many games, but their fans are very loyal!

5 _____

So whether you are a gourmet, a music fan, or a sports fan, you will find that Chicago is – in the words of the famous song – "One town that won't let you down."

2 Match the definitions with a word or phrase from the text.

The number of people who live in a place (paragraph 1)   population

1 Creates warm feelings (paragraph 1, three words)
2 Foreigners who come to live in the country (paragraph 2)
3 Arrived in large numbers (paragraph 3)
4 Places where people play and watch sports events (paragraph 4)
5 A food lover (paragraph 5)
6 Disappoint you (paragraph 5, three words)

3 Read the text again and correct the mistake in each sentence.

Few people think Chicago is a great city.
Most people think Chicago is a great city.

1 People in Chicago are famous for **hating** meat.
2 The Chicago Blues Festival is in the **winter**.
3 The Chicago Bears are a **basketball** team.

16

Vocabulary

American English and British English

1 Look at the picture. Listen and repeat the British English words (1–12).

2 Match the British English words (1–12) in exercise 1 with the American English words (a–l) in the box below.

- a) cookies
- b) movie theater
- c) chips
- d) first floor
- e) elevator
- f) cell phone
- g) sidewalk
- h) line
- i) store
- j) candy
- k) cab
- l) subway

1 underground = l) subway

LEARN THIS!

There are some differences between American and British spelling.

American	British
center	centre
theater	theatre
favorite	favourite
color	colour

3 First, complete the paragraph about Joe in American English. Then, complete the paragraph in British English! Use the words in the boxes.

American English
~~apartment~~   fall   gas
freeways   movies   vacation

British English
autumn   films   ~~flat~~   holiday
motorways   petrol

My friend Joe is very rich. He lives in a fabulous apartment/flat in New York. There's a room where he watches the latest Hollywood **(1)** ___ . Joe loves driving along the **(2)** ___ in his Cadillac. It uses a lot of **(3)** ___ . Joe always has a **(4)** ___ in Hawaii in the **(5)** ___ . This year, I'm going with him!

WORD LIST page 92

Writing — Building sentences

Writing about places

1 Read the model sentences and underline the adjectives. Then, put the adjectives in the correct groups (1–6).

MODEL SENTENCES
1. My <u>favorite</u> place is Cambridge, England.
2. Cambridge is an attractive, small city in the east of England.
3. The east of England is an important agricultural area.
4. Cambridge has a famous, ancient university.
5. The city has many old, gray, stone buildings.

1 quality	2 size	3 age
favorite	_____	_____
_____		
_____		
4 color	**5 material**	**6 type**
_____	_____	_____

2 Put the adjectives in the correct place in each sentence.

Cambridge has a river. (lovely)
Cambridge has a lovely river.

1. Punting on the river is a pastime. (popular)
2. Cambridge has summers. (warm, dry)
3. Tourism is the industry in Cambridge. (biggest)
4. There are also a lot of industries. (new, hi-tech)

 **tip!** When you are writing sentences, use different *types of adjectives*. If you use two or three adjectives to describe the same noun, check that your adjectives are in the correct order.

3 Write sentences. Put each group of adjectives + noun in their correct order (quality, size, age, color, material, type).

1. Boston is a / city / historical / famous
2. Amherst is a / small / town / lovely
3. What an / new / building / white / awful
4. It's an / industrial / ugly / region
5. Look at that / glass / skyscraper / tall
6. Visit this / ocean / beautiful / resort / tiny

1 Boston is a famous, historical city.

Your writing task

4 Write six sentences about one of the titles below. Include some examples of adjectives + noun.

My favorite place.
The place where I was born.
The place of my dreams.
The place where I live.

COMMUNICATION ACTIVITY 1
Student A turn to page 72   Student B turn to page 75

18

Song — Good Thing

1. Listen and put the lines (a–d) and (e–h) in their correct order (1–4) and (5–8). 🎧
2. How many examples of the present perfect are there in the song? Remember to include affirmative, negative, and question forms!
3. How do you say *You've been gone too long* in your language?

Good Thing

The one good thing
In my life
Has gone away
I don't know why

a) I don't know where
b) Follow her
c) Somewhere I can't
d) She's gone away

The one good thing
Didn't stay too long
My back was turned
And she was gone

e) Where have you gone?
f) You've been gone too long
g) Good thing
h) My good thing

PROGRESS REVIEW: UNITS 1 and 2

Difficult ☹ OK 😐 Easy! 🙂

Communication
- possession   (Whose ...?)
- offers and replies   (Would ...?)

Grammar
- simple past   (We, enjoyed ...)
- present perfect   (I have visited ...)
- relative pronouns   (who, that)
- whose   (He was a writer whose plays include Hamlet.)

Vocabulary
- American and British English

3 An American deli.

At Katz's delicatessen in Manhattan.

Meg Where's Jet? We've been here for an hour, since eight o'clock!
Tom Look! He's coming in now.
Meg There's a girl with him!
Tom Oh, that's Bella. She's crazy about him.
Meg Oh, really? Who's the guy behind her?
Tom Bud, Bella's brother. He's a sports fanatic. Big muscles, small brain.
Meg You're *jealous*, Tom! I think he's cute.
Jet Hi, Tom. Sorry I'm late. Apologies, Meg. You look great!
Meg Thanks. And you do, too.
Bella Hello, Meg. You're from England, right?
Meg Yes. How did you know?
Bella Jet's already told me a lot about you.
Meg Oh, I see.
Tom Let's order. Would you all like soda?
Bella Thanks.
Bud Sure.
Meg I'd prefer a juice, please.
Jet And I'd rather have coffee. Let's eat quickly, and then go to *Club 42*.
Bella But Jet! We've just arrived! It's early. We can go to the club later.
Meg *Club 42*? What's it like?
Jet I haven't been yet. But people say it's really cool.

Later, on the subway, going home …

Meg Jet dances very well.
Bud Yeah. He can sing and dance and act. He wants to go to drama school. But his dad won't let him.
Meg Why not?
Bud He'd prefer Jet to have a safe, secure job, like an accountant or a lawyer.
Meg Oh, boring!

Comprehension

1 Correct the mistake in each sentence.

Meg and **Jet** arrived at nine o'clock.
Meg and **Tom** arrived at nine o'clock.

1 Bella is crazy about **Tom**.
2 Bud is **Jet's** brother.
3 **Bella** wants to eat quickly, and go to *Club 42*.
4 **Tom** wants to go to drama school.
5 Jet's **mom** would prefer Jet to have a safe, secure job.

What's your opinion?
Why does Meg say Tom is jealous?

2 Who says these expressions?

She's crazy about him. Tom

1 You look great! _____
2 What's it like? _____
3 But his dad won't let him. _____

How do you say these expressions in your language?

Communication

Preferences

3 Listen and repeat. Then, ask and answer with a partner.

Boy Would you like a hamburger and a coffee?
Girl No, thanks. I'd prefer a cheeseburger and a soda.

Girl Would you like to be an engineer?
Boy No. I'd prefer to be a doctor.

Girl Would you like to visit New York?
Boy No. I'd rather visit London.

LEARN THIS!

I'd prefer a coffee.
= I'd prefer + noun
I'd prefer to have a coffee.
= I'd prefer + infinitive **with** to
I'd rather have a coffee.
= I'd rather + infinitive **without** to

Apologies

4 Listen and repeat. Then, practice with a partner. Use the Communication box to help you.

Boy Ouch! You've hurt my arm!
Girl Oh, I'm sorry.

Girl That's my newspaper!
Boy Oh, I apologize.

Communication	
Problems/Complaints	**Apologies**
You've taken my …	Sorry.
I was reading that …	Oh, I'm very sorry.
Hey! That's my …	I'm really sorry.
Ouch! Don't …	I apologize.

Pronunciation

The sounds /æ/, /e/ and /ɔ/

5 Listen and repeat.

/æ/	/e/	/ɔ/
man	said	coffee
thanks	well	ball
haven't	Bella	tall

The sounds of poetry

6 Listen and repeat. Practice reading the poem aloud.

"You are old, Father William,"
the young m<u>a</u>n s<u>a</u>id,
  "And your hair has become very white!
And yet you inc<u>e</u>ssantly[1] st<u>a</u>nd <u>o</u>n your h<u>ea</u>d.
  Do you think, <u>a</u>t your age, it is right?"

Lewis Carroll (1832–1898)

1 = often repeated

Grammar

Present perfect with *for* and *since*

1 First, study the examples. Then, complete the rules with *for* and *since*.

> I've lived in London since 1995.

> I've lived in London for fourteen years.

 **rules**

We use ___ with a period of time.
a year, two months, a week
We use ___ with a point in time.
2001, last Sunday, two o'clock

2 Complete the sentences about you, your friends, and your family.

1 I've studied English since _____ .
So I've studied English for _____ .

2 X has been my best friend since _____ .
She/He has been my best friend for _____ .

3 My parents/grandparents/aunt and uncle have lived here since _____ . So they have lived here for _____ .

3 Complete the paragraph about Eddie and Carmen. Use *for* and *since*.

Eddie and Carmen have been friends since the year 2002. So they have been friends for a long time. They are both on their school chess team. The team hasn't won a tournament **(1)** ___ months and months, **(2)** ___ June 2003 in fact!

But **(3)** ___ last December, Carmen has been the new team captain. She's been captain **(4)** ___ only a few months, but her team is improving. Carmen has given the team special coaching. They have played three games every day **(5)** ___ the past two weeks. **(6)** ___ last Saturday, the team has become determined to win their next tournament. That's because on Saturday they lost to a team from a rival school!

Present perfect with *just, already, yet*

4 First, translate Oscar's sentence into your language. Then, rearrange the words to make sentences.

> I can't come now. I've *just washed my hair.*

1 a chocolate milkshake. / Carmen / ordered / has / just
2 called / just / has / his friend. / Eddie
3 just / their final exams. / finished/ Eddie and Carmen / have

5 First, translate the dialog into your language. Then, complete the rules below. Use *just, yet,* and *already*.

Carmen Have you read the new Harry Potter book **yet**?

Eddie No, I haven't read the first Harry Potter book **yet**!

Carmen I've **already** read all the Harry Potter books twice!

 **rules**

We usually use ___ and ___ in **affirmative** sentences.
They go between *have / has* and the past participle.
We usually use ___ in **negative** sentences and **questions**.
It goes at the end of the sentence.

6 Complete the sentences with *already* or *yet*.

> No more cake for you! You've *already* had five pieces!

1 Mel's unhappy, because she hasn't finished her final exams ___ .
2 This CD is boring. We've ___ heard it three times.
3 Have you finished your homework ___ ?
4 She's ___ seen that movie. But she wants to see it again!

Adverbs of manner

7 First, study the examples. Then, complete the chart below.

Oscar sings **loudly**, but he talks **quietly**. Martine plays the guitar **well**, but she sings **badly**.

	adjective	adverb
Group 1 = + *ly*	bad	badly
	quick	(1) _____
	polite	(2) _____
Group 2 = ~~y~~ + *ily*	angry	angrily
	easy	(3) _____
	noisy	(4) _____
Group 3 = + *ally*	tragic	tragically
	fantastic	(5) _____
Group 4 = no change	early	early
	fast	(6) _____
	hard	(7) _____
	late	(8) _____
Group 5 = *irregular*	good	well

8 Complete the sentences. Change the adjectives into adverbs. Use the chart in exercise 7 to help you.

Our teacher speaks English _____ (quick).
Our teacher speaks English *quickly*.

1. He speaks Spanish _____ . (good)
2. Our train arrived _____ . (late)
3. The movie ended _____ . (dramatic)
4. The car stopped _____ . (sudden)
5. She interrupted me _____ . (rude)
6. The baby smiled _____ . (happy)

GRAMMAR HELP! pages 85–86

Study skills

Are you a good language learner?

9 Complete the questionnaire. Compare your scores with your friends' scores.

Are you a good language learner?

For each question, circle the correct answer and score for you!

Do you ….	never ☹	sometimes 😐	often ☺
1 speak English in class?	0	1	2
2 study English grammar rules?	0	1	2
3 use a monolingual dictionary?	0	1	2
4 do your homework on time?	0	1	2
5 make lists of your mistakes?	0	1	2
6 correct your mistakes?	0	1	2
7 learn new words every week?	0	1	2
8 listen to songs in English?	0	1	2
9 study for tests and exams?	0	1	2
10 study English during the vacations?	0	1	2
Your total score	……		

KEY

15–20 Congratulations! You are a good language learner.
6–14 OK! You are an average language learner, but you can improve.
0–5 Danger! You need to improve.

4 Famous Americans.

Reading

1 Read about the life of Martin Luther King. Use the dates to help you arrange the paragraphs (A–E) in their correct order (1–5). Then, listen and check your answers.

Order	1	2	3	4	5
Paragraph	C	_	_	_	_

A Injustice in the south
Like all black people in the southern states, Dr. King grew up in a world of discrimination, segregation, and injustice. In the 1950s, many schools were for white children only. They did not admit black children. Black people could not eat in the same restaurants, drink at the same water fountains, or sit on the same bus seats as white people.

B A violent end
In 1964, aged thirty-five, Dr. King won the Nobel Peace Prize. In the same year, President Lyndon Johnson signed the Civil Rights Act, which declared racial discrimination to be illegal. Then, four years later, while he was visiting Memphis, Tennessee, a gunman shot Dr. King through the head. The nation mourned.

C Early life
Martin Luther King was born on January 15, 1929, in Atlanta, Georgia. His father was a church minister, and his mother was a teacher. At school he was a very smart student, and he went to college in 1944, when he was only fifteen. He became a Doctor of Philosophy in 1955, and accepted a job as a minister of an Alabama church.

D Commemorating a hero
He was only thirty-nine when he died, but his achievements were considerable. In 1986 the government declared a national vacation in his honor. Now, on the third Monday of every January, the people of the United States officially commemorate the life and work of this American hero.

E Spreading the word
All that began to change in 1956, when Dr. King led the Civil Rights movement in a peaceful boycott of the buses in Montgomery, Alabama. Non-violent protest against racial discrimination spread all over the USA. There was a lot of resistance from the authorities. The police arrested Dr. King more than thirty times during the 1950s!

2 Complete the notes about the major events in the life of Dr. Martin Luther King.

Major events in the life of Dr. Martin Luther King

1929	born, Atlanta Georgia
1944	
1955	
1956	
1964	
1968	

3 Read the text again. Make a list of six new words and their meanings. Compare your list with your partner's list.

1 _____
2 _____
3 _____
4 _____
5 _____
6 _____

Vocabulary

Feelings and emotions

1 Listen. Write the correct feeling and emotion for each picture (1–8). Use the nouns in the box.

> anger   confidence   ~~envy~~   fear   happiness   jealousy
> pride   sadness

1 envy

5 _____

2 _____

6 _____

3 _____

7 _____

4 _____

8 _____

2 Match the nouns in exercise 1 (1–8) with their adjectives (a–h).

a) proud   e) jealous
b) angry   f) sad
c) envious   g) confident
d) happy   h) afraid

Feelings and emotions

nouns   adjectives

1 envy   =   c) envious

2 _____   _____

3 Listen. Circle the correct answers to the questions about feelings and emotions.

1 **Girl** Are you afraid of any animals or insects?
  Boy Yes. I'm afraid of *spiders*/*snakes*.

2 **Boy** What makes you feel happy?
  Girl I feel happy when I win a game of *tennis/soccer*.

3 **Girl** Have you ever felt envious?
  Boy Yes. I felt envious when my friend got a new *CD player/computer* for her birthday.

4 **Boy** What makes you feel angry?
  Girl I feel angry when my dad tells me to go to bed *early/before eleven o'clock*.

WORD LIST — page 92

Writing — Building paragraphs

Writing about movies and books

1 Read the model paragraph from a class project. What is the main topic of the paragraph? Choose from A–D.

- A The characters
- B The story
- C Why this is our favorite book
- D The author

MODEL PARAGRAPH

Our favorite book is *Harry Potter and the Sorcerer's Stone*. The story is about a young orphan boy called Harry Potter who lives with his horrible aunt, uncle, and cousin. When he is ten, Harry leaves them and goes to a school called Hogwarts, where he studies wizardry. The story is exciting, funny, and scary. We also like the movie, because the special effects are really great.

 **tip!** When you are writing paragraphs, check that all your sentences in each paragraph are about the same main topic.

2 Match two sentences from the students' project (1–6) with each paragraph topic (A–C).

- A The author
- B The story
- C The characters

1. Voldemort is a wicked, evil wizard who killed Harry's parents.
2. When she wrote the book, JK Rowling was unemployed and quite poor.
3. Quidditch is a really exciting team game, but the rules are very complicated!
4. At Hogwart's school, Harry learns to care for magical creatures, to make potions, and to cast spells.
5. Harry really likes Ron and Hermione, who also go to Hogwart's school.
6. She lived in Edinburgh and she wrote in a café.

3 Read the final paragraph of the project. What is its main topic? Which sentence should NOT be in the paragraph?

Harry Potter and the Sorcerer's Stone is our favorite book and movie for three reasons. First, there are a lot of unusual human and animal characters, such as Fluffy, the dog with three heads. Second, the story is very dramatic and exciting. The *Harry Potter* books have made the author, JK Rowling, very rich. Finally, it's our favorite because at the end Harry finds the magical sorcerer's stone before his enemies find it. Hooray! Three cheers for Harry Potter!

Your writing task

4 Write ONE paragraph about your favorite book or movie. In your paragraph, write about ONE topic. Use the paragraphs on this page, and these ideas to help you.

| The story | The author |
| The characters | Why this is my favorite |

COMMUNICATION ACTIVITY 2
Student A turn to page 72   Student B turn to page 75

Song   What Have I Done to Deserve This?

1 Listen and complete the song. Use the words in the box.

books   day   drinks (x2)   flowers (x2)
hours   love   money   nothing

2 Listen to the song again. How many times do you hear *What have I*?

3 How do you say *How am I gonna get through?* in your language?

What Have I Done to Deserve This?

I come here looking for money
Got to have it
And end up living with (1) _____
Oh, oh
Now you left me with (2) _____
Can't take it

How am I gonna get through?
How am I gonna get through?

I bought you (3) _____ , I brought you
(4) _____ I read you (5) _____ and talked for
(6) _____ Every (7) _____ so many
(8) _____ Such pretty (9) _____ , so tell me
What have I done to deserve this?

Since you went away I'm just hanging around,
And I'm wondering why I'm feeling down.
You went away, it should make me feel better,
But I don't know, oh, oh

How I'm gonna get through.
How I'm gonna get through.

PROGRESS REVIEW: UNITS 3 and 4

		Difficult ☹	OK 😐	Easy! ☺
Communication				
• Preferences	(I'd prefer / rather)	☐	☐	☐
Grammar				
Present perfect with				
• *for* and *since*	(since 2005, for a year)	☐	☐	☐
• *just*	(I've just finished …)	☐	☐	☐
• *already*	(She's already left)	☐	☐	☐
• *yet*	(We haven't seen it yet)	☐	☐	☐
• Adverbs	(loudly / well).	☐	☐	☐
Vocabulary				
• feelings and emotions		☐	☐	☐

Review: Units 1 to 4

Grammar

Present perfect and simple past

1 Complete the conversation. Use the present perfect or the simple past.

Tina Who is that boy over there? (**I never see**) I've never seen him before.
Mark You haven't? That's Tony Martinez. (**He start**) He started here in February.
Tina (**1 you ever meet**) him?
Mark Yes, of course. He's in my class. (**2 We study**) together for the spring tests last month.
Tina (**3 you pass**) the tests?
Mark I didn't, but Tony did. He is a very good student. (**4 He never fail**) a test in his life.
Tina Umm … does he have a girlfriend?
Mark I don't know, Tina. (**5 We never talk**) about things like that!

Relative pronouns who, which/that, and whose

2 Join the sentences with *which / that*, *who*, or *whose*.

> A modem is a machine. It connects a computer to the Internet.
> A modem is a machine which / that connects a computer to the Internet.

1 A burglar is a thief. He steals things from houses.
2 Chimpanzees are animals. They are closely related to humans.
3 Leonardo DiCaprio is an actor. His most famous movie is *Titanic*.
4 Composers are people. They write music.
5 Tony Martinez is a boy. His test scores are always good.
6 Reggae is a type of music. It started in the Caribbean.

Present perfect with *for* and *since*

3 Complete the paragraph. Use *for* and *since*.

Jenny and I have been on this beach for nearly three hours. It is very quiet – we haven't seen another person since 11 o'clock this morning. I have come to this same beach every year (**1**) ___ I was fourteen, when I first discovered it. Jenny hasn't known about it (**2**) ___ that long. I brought her here on the day we met, and she has returned with me every year (**3**) ___ then. She loves it! We have been together (**4**) ___ three years now, and we often talk about the times we have had here on the beach.

Present perfect with *just*, *already*, and *yet*

4 Complete the sentences with *just*, *already*, or *yet*.

He has *just* sat on the cat!

1 No, not that CD. I've ___ heard it. Sonia played it for me last week.

2 He hasn't decided what to order ___.

3 He looks as if he has ___ won the lottery!

Vocabulary

American English and British English

5 Complete the lists. Use the words in the box.

> candy chips crisps ~~movie theater~~
> petrol sidewalk underground

American English		British English
movie theater	=	cinema
1 chips	=	_____
2 _____	=	pavement
3 gas	=	_____
4 _____	=	sweets
5 subway	=	_____

6 Complete the words. Add consonants to the American words and vowels to the British words.

American	/	British
1 c a b	/	t a x i
2 _ i _ e	/	q _ _ _ _
3 _ _ o _ e	/	_ _ o _ e
4 _ o o _ i e _	/	b _ sc _ _ t s
5 e _ e _ a _ o _	/	l _ f t

Feelings and emotions

7 Change the nouns into adjectives and complete the sentences.

> anger envy fear ~~jealousy~~ pride

> My boyfriend is *jealous* because my new boss is very handsome.

1 I never travel by plane because I am _____ of flying.
2 Greg's parents were very _____ when he won first prize in the essay contest.
3 My neighbor has bought a beautiful new car. I am feeling very _____ .
4 Please don't be _____ . I didn't mean to annoy you.

8 Complete the puzzle.

Across
1 The American word for *holiday*.
4 British people put this in their cars.
6 The feeling that you can do well (noun).
8 American people put this in their cars.
9 A British person sees this at the movie theater.

Down
2 The British word for the season between summer and winter.
3 A _____ *theater* is the American word for *cinema*.
5 The opposite of happiness.
7 The American word for the season between summer and winter.

5 On Broadway!

It's Saturday morning on Broadway, the heart of New York's theater district.

Meg Look! That's where we have to get our tickets for tonight's show.
Jet Be careful! The sign says "Don't walk", that means you have to wait. You can't cross yet.
Tom In any case, we don't have to get the tickets now. I have to collect them from the theater, at seven.

Later, the three friends discuss Jet's problem with his father.

Jet If I go to drama school, I'll be a famous Broadway star one day!
Meg You'll need money for drama school! But if your dad doesn't approve, he won't give you any.
Jet Oh, yeah. It's impossible to go to drama school without money! So I'll have to get a job.
Tom What about a scholarship? If you get a scholarship, tuition is free!
Jet You're right! I'll write for an application form. But if my dad finds out, he'll be angry.
Meg So don't tell him!
Tom But that's dishonest Meg! Jet has to tell his dad.
Jet Meg's right. I don't have to tell Dad – not yet!

It's early evening. Bella and Bud are window-shopping with Meg.

Meg I need to buy something for my sister's birthday.
Bella Those designer scarves are great. But they're $150 each! That's incredible!
Meg Designer clothes aren't worth the extra money!
Bud Guys, we need to hurry. It's six-thirty!
Meg OK. I don't have to buy anything today. My sister will have to wait for her present!

Comprehension

1 Answer the questions.

Why does Meg have to be careful?
Because the sign says "Don't walk!"
1 Why does Tom have to be at the theater at seven o'clock?
2 Why will Jet need money?
3 Why will a scholarship help Jet?
4 Why is Meg window-shopping?

What's your opinion?
"So don't tell him!"
Do you agree with Meg? Why?/Why not?

2 Who says these expressions?

In any case Tom
1 one day _____
2 That's incredible! _____
3 Guys _____

How do you say these expressions in your language?

Communication

Obligation (*have to*) and prohibition (*can't*)

3 Listen and repeat. Then, ask and answer with a partner.

Girl What does this sign mean?
Boy It means you have to make a left.

Boy What does this sign mean?
Girl It means you can't feed the animals.

Obligation (*have to*) and lack of obligation (*don't have to*)

4 Listen and repeat. Then, ask and answer with a partner.

Girl At home, do you have to do the dishes?
Boy Yes, I do. And I have to clean my room!

Boy At school, do you have to study Latin?
Girl No, I don't. But I have to study English!

do the ironing   study chemistry
vacuum the carpets take a test every week

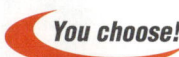

Pronunciation

Final consonants /ŋ/ /ŋk/; /s/ /z/

5 Listen and repeat.

/ŋ/	/ŋk/	/s/	/z/
knocking	think	tickets	is
sing	bank	cross	scarves
something	thank	dance	guys

The sounds of poetry

6 Listen and repeat. Practice reading the poem aloud.

"Is anybody there?" said the Traveler,
Knocking on the moonlit door;
And his horse in the silence champed[1] the grasses
Of the forest's ferny[2] floor
            Walter de la Mare (1873–1956)

[1] = ate   [2] = leafy

5

Grammar

Zero conditional

1 First, study the example. Then, answer the two questions below.

If CDs **become** very hot, they **melt**!

← *If* clause → ← main clause →

1 In zero conditionals, which tense do we use
   a) for the *If* clause?
   b) for the main clause?
2 Do we use zero conditionals to express facts or predictions about the future?

2 Match the *If* clauses (1–5) with the correct main clauses (a–e).

1 If I read for a long time,
2 If you eat a lot of sugar,
3 If you don't know English,
4 If I don't eat breakfast,
5 If you freeze water,

a) you can't get some jobs.
b) you get bad teeth.
c) it turns into ice.
d) I usually get a headache.
e) I always get hungry.

First conditional

3 First, study the examples. Then, answer the two questions below.

If I **pass** my science test, my mom **will buy** me a new computer game.

If I **don't pass** my test, my dad **won't let** me go to the REM concert next month.

1 In first conditionals, which tenses do we use
   a) for the *If* clause?
   b) for the main clause?
2 Do we use first conditionals to express facts or predictions about the future?

> **LEARN THIS!**
>
> When the **If clause** comes first, we use a comma. See Exercise 4 numbers 1, 3, 5. When the **main clause** comes first, you don't use a comma. See Exercise 4 numbers 2, 4, 6.

4 Choose the correct verbs.

If we *leave/will leave* now, we *don't miss/won't miss* the start of the movie.

If we leave now, we won't miss the start of the movie.

1 If it *rains/will* rain tomorrow, *we won't play/don't play* tennis.
2 Dad *is/will* be angry if I *will stay/stay* out after midnight.
3 If the bus *doesn't come/won't come* soon, we *are/will be* late.
4 Mom *isn't/won't be* pleased if I *don't pass/won't pass* my tests.
5 If you *walk/'ll walk* down this road, you *see/'ll see* the restaurant, on your left.
6 Our teacher *is/will be* very happy if we *answer/will answer* all these correctly!

have to

5 First, study the examples. Then, complete the chart below with the correct forms.

Eddie **has to** finish his homework before he watches TV.

Eddie and Carmen **don't have to** go to school tomorrow.

	affirmative (= obligation)	negative (= lack of obligation)
she/he/it	(1) _____	doesn't have to
I/we/you/they	have to	(2) _____

6 First, read the list of what Eddie and Carmen *have to* do, and *don't have to* do. Then, say whether the statements below are true or false.

	Eddie	Carmen
go to college on Fridays	✓	✓
feed the cat	✗	✓
make dinner	✓	✗
go to bed before 12 pm	✓	✓
do the shopping	✗	✓

Eddie and Carmen have to go to college on Fridays.   T
1. Eddie has to feed the cat.
2. Carmen doesn't have to make dinner.
3. Eddie and Carmen don't have to go to bed before 12 pm.
4. Carmen has to do the shopping.

need, have to and can't

7 Study the sentences (a–d) and their meanings. Then, answer the two questions below.

a) Oscar and Martine **have to** pay for the sun umbrella.
 = Paying for the sun umbrella is obligatory.
b) They **can't** swim here.
 = Swimming here is prohibited.
c) I **need to** use my sunblock.
 = Using sunblock is necessary.
d) We **don't have to** go home yet.
 = It isn't necessary to go home yet.
1 Which verb forms do require *to*?
2 Which verb form does not require *to*?

8 Choose the correct verbs.

You *need to / don't need to* take any warm clothes. The weather will be hot.
You *don't need to* take any warm clothes. The weather will be hot.

1 Astronomers *need to / don't have to* know about the solar system.
2 You *don't have to / can't* smoke in "No Smoking" areas.
3 You *have to / don't need to* bring any money, my dad will pay for us.
4 English teachers *have to / can't* know a lot about grammar.

LEARN THIS!

They **have** + to pay   I **need** + <u>to</u> use
You **can't** + ~~to~~ swim   He **needs** + <u>to</u> go
She **doesn't have** + to go   We **need** + <u>to</u> leave

GRAMMAR HELP!   pages 86–87

6 Welcome to Oz!

Reading

1 First, read and listen to the description of Australia. Then, choose the best picture (A–D) to illustrate each paragraph (1–4).

Paragraph   1   2   3   4
Picture   __ __ __ __

Title _____

1 WORLDS ANCIENT AND MODERN

Australia is a land of great geographical and cultural variety. Modern cities lie next to vast, untouched natural landscapes. Western culture dominates, but the ancient traditions of the Aborigines have not disappeared. **They** live on, both in the cities and in the Outback.

A

B

2 LIFE IN THE CITIES ...

Australia is a very urbanized society, with nearly 90% of **its** population living in the cities on the coast. These city-dwellers enjoy all the usual benefits of a modern, multi-cultural lifestyle – from restaurants, theaters, and museums, to rock concerts, night clubs, and street festivals. **They** have it all!

3 ... AND ON THE BEACH

In contrast to the social whirl of city life, there is beach culture. Aussies call the beach "the great leveler" because **it** is accessible to everyone, no matter what age or social class they are. During the summer, beach-lovers flock there to go surfing and snorkeling, to have picnics and, of course, to sunbathe. **Their** lives revolve around the beach at this time of year.

C

D

4 THE WORLD OF THE OUTBACK

But in Australia, you are never far from the wilderness of the Outback, and a completely different way of life. **Here** are the lands owned by the Aborigines, who have lived on this continent for over 50,000 years. **They** carry on their ancient traditions through a form of art and storytelling known as "The Dreaming". **This** is the world's oldest art form, and a unique part of Australian culture.

2 Find these words in the text. What do they refer to?

They (paragraph 1)
the ancient traditions of the Aborigines

1 its (paragraph 2)
2 They (paragraph 2)
3 it (paragraph 3)
4 Their (paragraph 3)
5 Here (paragraph 4)
6 They (paragraph 4)
7 This (paragraph 4)

3 Choose the best title for the text from (1–4) below.

1 The history of Australia
2 "The great leveler"
3 A land of contrasts
4 The culture of the Aborigines

Vocabulary

Word formation: prefixes

1 First, study the examples. Then, read sentences 1–4 and complete the chart of prefixes and words below.

John's bedroom is **tidy**.

Kathy's bedroom is **untidy**.

 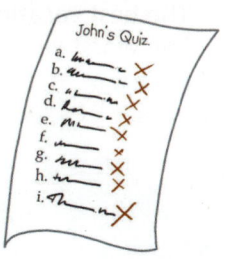

Kathy's answers are **correct**. John's answers are **incorrect**.

1 John's dog always does what he tells it. It's **obedient**.
  Kathy's dog never does what she tells it. It's **disobedient**.
2 On sunny days, it's **possible** to see the mountains.
  On cloudy days, it's **impossible** to see them.
3 *Stop* is a **regular** verb.
  Go is an **irregular** verb.
4 The speed limit is 40mph.
  Driving at 40 mph is **legal**.
  Driving at 140 mph is **illegal**.

prefix +	word	prefix +	word
un	tidy	in	correct
1 ___	___	3 ___	___
2 ___	___	4 ___	___

2 Complete the sentences (1–6) below. Then, listen and check your answers.

> **un**kind   **in**complete   **im**patient
> **dis**honest   **il**logical   ~~**in**visible~~
> **ir**replaceable

I've just read a great book called The **Invisible** Man. It's about a man you can't see.
1 She never tells the truth. She's ___ .
2 That was a terrible thing to say to her. You were very ___ . You should apologize.
3 You have to wait. Don't be so ___ .
4 This jigsaw is ___ . Some pieces are missing.
5 That antique vase is unique. It's ___ .
6 Your argument doesn't make sense. It's ___ .

3 Match each prefix (1–6) with two words in the list (a–l) to make new words. Use your dictionary to check your answers.

1	dis +	a)	dependent	g)	appear
2	il +	b)	agree	h)	moral
3	im +	c)	finite	i)	literate
4	in +	d)	mobile	j)	relevant
5	ir +	e)	pleasant	k)	logical
6	un +	f)	fortunate	l)	responsible

5 Write sentences to illustrate the meanings of the new words in exercise 3.

NEW WORDS!

1+b = disagree

I liked the movie but my friend disagreed. He said it was terrible.

1+g   dis…

WORD LIST   pages 93 and 95

Writing — Planning and making notes

Writing about vacations

1 First, read the model plan and notes. Then, answer the questions below.

MODEL PLAN AND NOTES

Title: My last vacation

A   Introduction: basic information
   when   last summer, July
   where San Francisco
   why   to improve my English
   who   with some classmates

B   Main part: what, when, where, etc.
   am   classes with strange, young teacher!
   pm   sports, visits to museums, parks
   eve parties, movies, TV with host family
   Sat/Sun excursions to Muir Woods, Monterey, Golden Gate Bridge

C   Conclusion: my opinions
   liked   Fisherman's Wharf, Alcatraz
   why   interesting, fabulous view
   didn't like food, noise, traffic
   why not Korean food better, pollution
   go again? Yes, I'd like to but not to a school, and on my own!

---

1 What's the **title** of the composition?
2 How many **paragraphs** will there be?
3 What is the main **topic** of each paragraph?

---

tip!
When you are planning a composition, follow these steps:
Step 1   Study the composition title.
Step 2   Make notes for *Introduction, Main part, Conclusion.*
Step 3   Add extra notes to each paragraph of your plan.

---

2 Add these extra notes to the correct paragraph of the plan.

a) didn't like the weather, because of rain
b) and with two of our teachers
c) the last Sunday – went to Alcatraz
d) liked American host family – kind, generous
e) on last eve special theater eve – saw Cats!
f) for two weeks

a) = C (Conclusion: my opinions)

Your writing task

3 Plan a composition about one of the titles below. Make notes for your Introduction, Main part and Conclusion. Compare your plans and notes with other students.

My last vacation
The best vacation I ever had
The worst vacation I ever had

COMMUNICATION ACTIVITY 3
Student A turn to page 73   Student B turn to page 76

Song — On Broadway

1. Listen and put the words in the first two lines of each verse in their correct order.

2. Who do you think *They* are in the song? Where do they live?

3. How do you say *I won't quit till I'm a star* in your language?

On Broadway

They say
   on Broadway" / bright / are / "The neon lights
They say
   in the air!" / always / "There's / magic
But when you're walkin' down the street
And you don't have enough to eat
The magic disappears and you're nowhere

They say
   are / "The girls / on Broadway" / oh so cool
They say
   the blues" / "The girls / don't give / there / you
But how am I gonna make some time?
When all I got is just one dime?
and just one dime won't even shine my shoes!

Ha! They say
   too long / "You / on Broadway" / won't last
   take / back home!" / "You'll / a Greyhound bus
They all say.
But oh! They're so wrong, I know they are
'Cause I can play this fine guitar
and I won't quit till I'm a star on Broadway!

PROGRESS REVIEW: UNITS 5 AND 6

		Difficult ☹	OK 😐	Easy! 😊
Communication				
• obligation and prohibition	(have to / need to).	☐	☐	☐
• lack of obligation	(don't have to study Latin).	☐	☐	☐
Grammar				
• zero conditional	(If ..., they melt)	☐	☐	☐
• first conditional	(If ..., she will buy)	☐	☐	☐
• have to	(I have to go)	☐	☐	☐
• can't and need	(you can't swim, we need to sleep)	☐	☐	☐
Vocabulary				
• prefixes	(*un*tidy, *in*correct)	☐	☐	☐

7 Champions.

Bella's cheerleading team is practicing for the final of the basketball championship.

Two four six eight
Who do we appreciate?
They're the best
They're the stars in the sky
They are the guys
From Lincoln High!
Gooooooooooooo Lions!

Meg How do you become a cheerleader, Bella?
Bella First, you fill out an application form with information about your name, age, and stuff. Then you're interviewed.
Meg Interviewed?
Bella Yes, you're interviewed by the sports teachers. Finally, you are given a routine to do, and if you're lucky, you're selected. I was chosen last year.
Meg Are boys ever chosen?
Jet I applied to be a cheerleader, but I wasn't even interviewed!
Tom Boy cheerleaders? Cheerleading is for girls, Jet.
Meg Don't be so sexist, Tom! Girls are allowed to play soccer so why can't boys be cheerleaders?
Bella Even Bud approves of male cheerleaders.
Meg Ah! Good for him!
Tom Bud? You can't be serious!
Bella It's true, Tom!

Two days later. It's the final game of the championship.

All Hooray. Lincoln are the champions!
Tom But look at Bud. He's been injured!
Jet He was pushed over by their number eight. After the final whistle!
Meg Has he been hurt?
Bella Don't worry. He'll be OK.
Meg Oh, I hope so. I'll go and help him.
Jet (whispers) Bella. I think Meg must be in love.

Comprehension

1 Put the events of the story (a–g) in their correct order (1–7).

Order 1 2 3 4 5 6 7
Events c __ __ __ __ __ __

a Lincoln High become the champions.
b Jet tells the story about his application to be a cheerleader.
c Bella practices with the other cheerleaders.
d Jet thinks that Meg must be in love.
e Bud is injured.
f Bella explains how cheerleaders are selected.
g Meg goes to help Bud.

What's your opinion?

Are some sports only for girls?
And are some sports only for boys?

2 Who says these expressions?

If you're lucky. Bella
1 Good for him! _____
2 You can't be serious. _____
3 Oh, I hope so. _____

How do you say these expressions in your language?

Communication

Logical deductions: *must be, can't be*

3 First, listen and repeat.

Lord Moorcroft is dead!
A Is that a bottle of poison?
B Yes. It must be.
A Why?
B Because it says "Do not drink".

B Is that a footprint?
A No. It can't be.
B Why not?
A Because it's tiny!

4 Now ask and answer with your fellow detective.

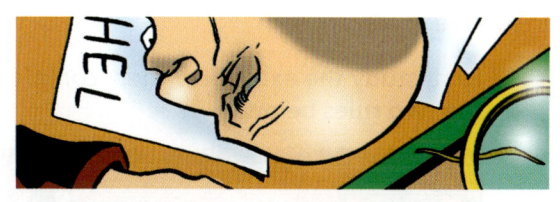

a message from the victim? some of Lord Moorcroft's hair?
✓ it says "HELP!" ✗ he didn't have any.

Sequence: *first ... then ... finally ...*

5 Listen and repeat. Then, ask and answer with a partner.

Boy How do you think people become successful movie stars?
Girl First, they go to Hollywood.
Then, they go for auditions.
Finally, they get a part in a movie!

successful pop stars
successful soccer players

You choose!

Pronunciation

The sounds /ɪ/, /e/ and /ʊ/

6 Listen and repeat.

/ɪ/	/e/	/ʊ/
h<u>ere</u>	th<u>ere</u>	p<u>ure</u>
cheerl<u>ea</u>der	f<u>air</u>	r<u>ur</u>al
cl<u>ear</u>	c<u>are</u>	c<u>ure</u>

The sounds of poetry

7 Listen and repeat. Practice reading the poem aloud.

The cat went h<u>ere</u> and th<u>ere</u>
And the moon spun round like a top,
And the n<u>ear</u>est friend of the moon,
The creeping cat, looked up.
Black Minnaloushe stared at the moon,
For, wander and wail[1] as he would,
The p<u>ure</u> cold light in the sky
Troubled his animal blood.

WB Yeats (1865–1939)

[1] to cry

7

Grammar

Passive

1 First, study the examples. Then, complete the two rules below.

active = *to make*
They **make** pop videos here. (simple present)
They **made** Madonna's last video. (simple past)

passive = *to be made*
Pop videos **are made** here. (simple present passive)
Madonna's last video **was made** here. (simple past passive)

rules
1 The *object* in active sentences, becomes the _____ in passive sentences.
2 The *main verb* in active sentences becomes _____ + the *past participle of the main verb* in passive sentences.

2 Read the sentences. Identify the *subject* and the *passive verb* in each one.

Most pop videos | are produced | in the USA.
   subject   passive verb

1 Madonna's video was made last week.
2 Pop videos are shown every night.

3 Change the active sentences into passive.

How a pop video is made:

First, they choose a singer and a song.
First, a singer and a song *are chosen*.
1 Then, they select a location.
2 Next, they arrange the lighting and sound.
3 After that, they rehearse everything.
4 Then, they film the video.
5 Finally, they add the song to the video.

Passive with *by* + agent

LEARN THIS!

We use the passive with **by + agent** when it's important to know who does the action.
Satellite TV is watched **by millions of people**.

4 Rearrange the words and phrases to make passive sentences with *by* + agent.

Satellite TV and soccer. How does it work?

are filmed / games / by TV companies. / First,
First, games are filmed by TV companies.

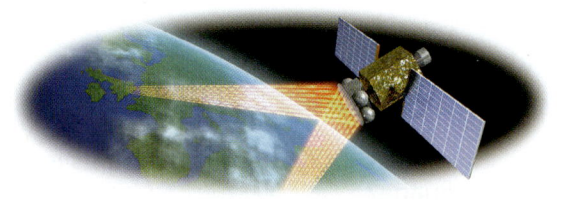

1 pictures / around the world / Then, / by satellites. / are sent

2 on the ground. / Next, / by large antennae / are received / pictures

3 to our homes / the pictures / by cable or digital signals. / are transmitted / Finally, /

40

5 Complete the newspaper article. Use the simple past passive.

CROCODILE DRAMA!

Crockie the croc says, "I want to go home."

At midnight last night, a large crocodile (**see**) was seen in the middle of New York! The police (**call**) were called by a young woman who saw it. The woman and her friend (**1 interview**) by the police. But their amazing story (**2 not believe**).

But at six o'clock this morning a crocodile (**3 report**) to be at a subway station! It was trying to get on a subway to JFK airport.

Eventually, the croc (**4 catch**) by staff from the Bronx zoo. They said, "His name is Crockie. He (**5 bring**) here from Africa. He's escaped twice this year. His mate (**6 send**) back to Africa last year. We think he wants to go too."

Logical deductions: *must be, can't be*

6 Study the examples. Then, complete the sentences below. Use *must be* or *can't be*.

He hasn't eaten all day.
He **must be** hungry.

You've just eaten a pound of meat.
You **can't be** hungry!

1 You've been in bed for twelve hours! Get up! You _____ tired!
2 She's dating Steve? But he's horrible! She _____ crazy.
3 They won the gold medal. They _____ proud.
4 Did you really like that terrible movie? You _____ serious!

GRAMMAR HELP! page 88

Study skills

How do you practice English?

7 Read what the students say. Do you practice English in the same ways?

> I have an e-mail friend in London.

1 Suki from Japan

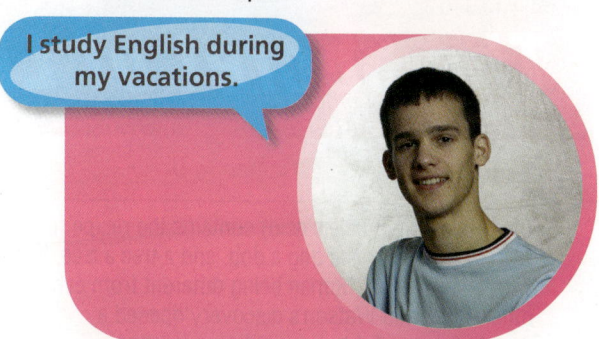

> I study English during my vacations.

2 Ramiro, from Argentina

> We talk in English for ten minutes every day.

3 Teresa and Carlos, from Brazil

8 Which THREE methods of practicing English does your group think are the most useful? Compare your opinions with other groups.
1 Talking in English with your friends.
2 Making English labels for things.
3 Reading English magazines.
4 Having an English-speaking e-mail/pen pal.
5 Watching English movies and TV programs.
6 Studying English during the vacations.
Other ...

In our opinion, the three most useful methods of practicing English are ...

You choose!

8 The secret of life.

Reading

1 Read the text. Match the topics (1–5) with the paragraphs (A–E) to put the paragraphs in their correct order. Then, listen and check your answers.

1. The discovery — Paragraph D
2. What is DNA? _____
3. Feeding the world _____
4. Dolly the sheep _____
5. A question of ethics _____

2 Read the text again and answer the questions.

1. When did Crick and Watson discover the structure of DNA?
2. Where did they first announce their discovery?
3. What is a possible result of GM crops mixing with natural species?
4. What was the name of the first cloned sheep?

The Secret of Life

A _____
DNA (deoxyribonucleic acid) contains the recipe for life. DNA is what makes a dog a dog, and a tree a tree. It is what makes every human being different from every other. Crick and Watson's discovery opened a wonderful new field of scientific exploration.

B _____
Animals, too, are part of the DNA revolution. In 1997, scientists used a technique called cloning to create Dolly – a sheep which was an exact copy of its mother! We can now clone an infinite number of the very best farm animals. There are even companies which, for a fee, will clone your beloved pet for you!

C _____
But is cloning right? Or are scientists playing God? Crick and Watson's gift to humanity was incredibly valuable, but it has raised some serious ethical questions.

D _____
"We have found the secret of life!" These words were spoken by Francis Crick in a Cambridge pub in February, 1953. And in many ways it was true. Crick and his partner, James Watson, told their scientific colleagues about their discovery. It was the double-helix structure of DNA.

E _____
It has revolutionized agriculture. Genetically modified (GM) crops are used throughout the world. Many people believe GM technology will bring an end to world hunger. It will be possible, for example, to produce crops which can grow in the desert. But others are worried that the DNA from GM crops might mix with natural species and produce "Frankenstein" plants which cannot be controlled.

Discussion

3 What's your opinion?
Do you think that cloning and/or genetic modification is a good thing or a bad thing? Give reasons for your opinion.

Vocabulary

Word formation: suffixes

1 First, check that you understand the meanings of the words (1–8). Then, listen and add the correct suffix to each word. 🎧

SUFFIXES
-ation -ese -ian -ion -ish
-ment -ness

verb	+ suffix
agree	agree**ment**
1 collect	_____
2 embarrass	_____
3 entertain	_____
4 inform	_____
adjective	**+ suffix**
dark	dark**ness**
5 kind	_____
6 smooth	_____
noun	**+ suffix**
Pole	Pol**ish**
7 Japan	_____
8 Egypt	_____

Did you notice?
When you add a suffix, the part of speech may change
from verb to noun   agree → agree**ment**
from adjective to noun dark → dark**ness**
from noun to adjective Pole → Pol**ish**

2 Complete each sentence with a word + suffix from exercise 1.

His dad has an enormous stamp collection.
1 After sunset _____ came.
2 He lived in Tokyo, and he speaks _____ really well.
3 Yes, Ahmed is _____ He comes from Cairo.
4 I went to the travel agent and got some _____ about vacations in England.

3 Study the groups of words (1–6). Choose the correct meaning of the suffix in each group. Use the meanings in the box.

~~Abstract ideas~~ Being "full of" Being "without" Female Occupation People and ideas

1 Abstract ideas   2 _____   3 _____
commun**ism**   commun**ist**   farm**er**
sex**ism**   sex**ist**   teach**er**
social**ism**   social**ist**   photograph**er**

4 _____   5 _____   6 _____
actr**ess**   help**ful**   help**less**
lion**ess**   hope**ful**   hope**less**
waitr**ess**   use**ful**   use**less**

4 Choose ONE word from each group in exercise 3. Write sentences to illustrate their meanings. Use your dictionary to help you, if necessary.

Group 1
Socialism is a political ideal.

5 Match each word (1–8) with one of the suffixes (a–h) to make new words. Use your dictionary to check your answers.

words	suffixes
1 art	a) -ee
2 box	b) -er
3 capital	c) -ess
4 disappoint	d) -ful
5 employ	e) -ism
6 faith	f) -ist
7 penny	g) -less
8 priest	h) -ment

The spelling of one word changes. Which one?

6 Write sentences to illustrate the meanings of the new words in exercise 5.

New words
1 +f = artist
My sister draws and paints really well. She wants to be an artist.

WORD LIST   pages 93 and 95

8

Writing — Expanding plans and notes

Writing about jobs

1 First, compare the plan and notes with the final model introduction. Then, complete the chart below.

```
Title: My drm job
Introduction: info about me
job name: flight attendt
how long: have wanted for 3 yrs, since Phil
why: 'cos love travlg & meetg peop fm difft counts
```

MODEL INTRODUCTION

My dream job

My dream job is to be a flight attendant. I have wanted to be a flight attendant for three years, since my big brother Philip became one. I want to be a flight attendant because I love traveling and meeting people from different countries.

Chart of differences!

Plan/notes	Model introduction
drm	dream
1 info	_____
2 attendt	_____
3 'cos	_____
4 frm	_____
5 difft counts	_____

2 Complete the chart. Match the notes (1–4) with these words: *advantage, height, interested, physical, opinion*.

physic	physical
1 ht	_____
2 int'd in	_____
3 advs	_____
4 op	_____

Now choose your notes for these words (5–8).

educn	education
5 _____	important
6 _____	especially
7 _____	conclusion
8 _____	disadvantages

tip! When you expand your plans and notes into full sentences and paragraphs, remember to check your final work, especially the *grammar*, *vocabulary*, *spelling*, and *punctuation*!

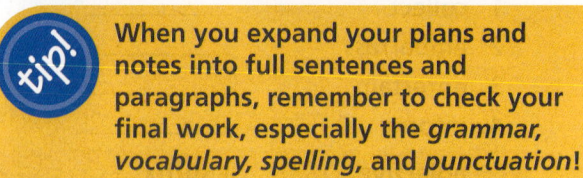

3 Expand the plan and notes into full sentences and paragraphs.

```
Main part:   job requirements
physical     age: have to be 18+.
             height: need to be 5'5"–6'2"
education    school grades imp, esp geog &
             math.
             langs: Engl essential!
personality  have to be friendly, polite, etc.
             need to be interested peop
Conclusion   advantages & disadvantages
advs         trav, meet peop, make new friends.
disadvs      long hours, away fm home a lot
my opinion   best job in world!
```

Main part

To be a flight attendant, you have to be eighteen years old. You need to be between 5'5" and 6'2" tall. School grades …

Your writing task

4 Make a plan and write notes about "My dream job". Then, expand your notes into three paragraphs.

COMMUNICATION ACTIVITY 4
Student A turn to page 73   Student B turn to page 76

Song — When Will I be Loved?

2 Listen and complete the song. Use the words and phrases in the box.

> cheated   lied to   ~~made blue~~
> mistreated   pushed 'round
> turned down

2 How many different examples of the passive are there in the song?

2 How do you say *She always breaks my heart* in your language?

When Will I be Loved?

I've been made blue, I've been (1) _____ ,
When will I be loved?
I've been (2) _____ , I've been (3) _____
When will I be loved?

When I meet a new girl
That I want for mine
She always breaks my heart in two,
It happens every time

I've been (4) _____ , been (5) _____
When will I be loved?

PROGRESS REVIEW: UNITS 7 and 8

	Difficult ☹	OK 😐	Easy! 🙂
Communication			
• logical deductions *(must be / can't be)*	☐	☐	☐
• sequence *(first … then … finally …)*	☐	☐	☐
Grammar			
• passive *(CDs are made here.)*	☐	☐	☐
• logical deduction	☐	☐	☐
Vocabulary			
• with suffixes *(agree**ment**, collec**tion**)*	☐	☐	☐

Review: Units 5 to 8

Grammar

Zero and first conditional

1 Study the sentences (a–d) Then, answer the questions (1–4) below.

a If you divide fifteen by five, you get three.
b If you heat water to 212°F, it boils.
c If you eat all the candy, you'll be sick.
d If he knows you're coming to the party, he'll come too.

1 Which two sentences use the simple present in the main clause?
2 Which two sentences use the future with *will*?
3 Which two sentences express facts?
4 Which two sentences express predictions about the future?

2 Choose the correct verbs.

If it doesn't stop snowing, they *close/will close* the college for the day.

1 If we don't hurry up, all the tickets *are/will be* sold.
2 If she stays up late at night, Sue always *gets/will get* very tired. 
3 If you *won't/don't* feed fish, they die. 
4 If it *isn't/won't be* expensive, she will buy it. 

can't, have to, and don't have to

3 Complete the sentences with *can't*, *have to*, or *don't have to*.

Dear Mark
I'm really enjoying life at college! Of course, I *don't have to* wear a uniform, which is nice. But the best thing is, I can concentrate on my favorite subject – English! I (1) _____ study math or chemistry now! OK, there's a lot of work to do – we (2) _____ write an essay every week. There are a lot of lectures, too, and we (3) _____ miss any of them because they are all important.
   I live in a student house near the college, so I (4) _____ get up too early in the morning. Unfortunately, I (5) _____ walk there every day because my bicycle was stolen last week. You (6) _____ forget to lock your bike when you come to visit me, or the same will happen to you!
Best wishes,
Tina

Logical deductions: must be, can't be

4 Complete the conversations with *must be* or *can't be*.

I paid $10,000 for this car.
You *must be* joking!

1 I'm exhausted.
   You _____ exhausted. You haven't done any work all day!
2 Sue failed every test this year.
   Her parents _____ very angry.
3 I've just seen Steve in the library.
   Then he _____ on vacation in Mexico!
4 My dad bought a new computer for my little brother.
   You _____ envious.

46

Passive

5 Complete the article from a student newspaper. Use the simple past passive.

Congratulations Suzanne!

Last week Suzanne Rogers (**award**) was awarded first prize in the Student Scientist of the Year contest. The prize (**1 present**) by Professor Raskin of Harvard University. Suzanne's project (**2 choose**) from among 50 other entries, all of which (**3 produce**) by students between 15 and 18 years old. Hers (**4 admire**) a lot by the judges. "I (**5 give**) a lot of help by my teacher," she said shyly. "Winning this prize was a real shock. It (**6 not expect**)."

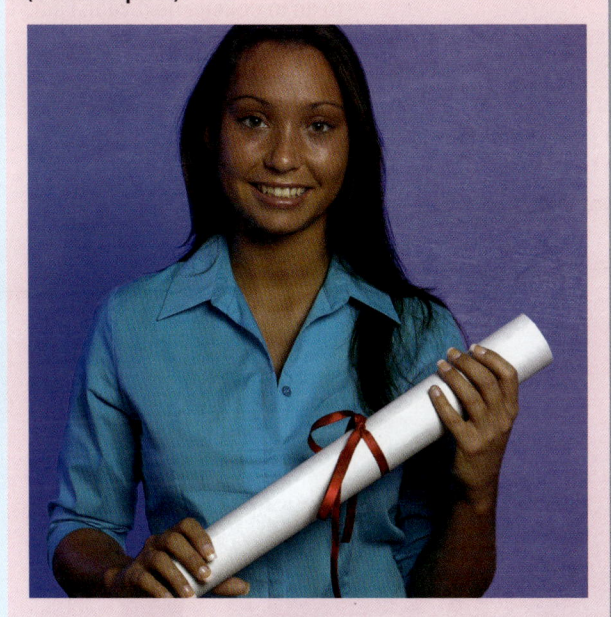

Vocabulary

Word formation: prefixes

6 Complete the words with *dis-*, *im-*, *in-*, or *un-* to form their opposites, and put them in the correct column.

| correct | honest | kind | mature |
| obedient | patient | usual | visible |

dis-	im-	in-	un-
dishonest	____	____	____
____	____	____	____

Word formation: suffixes

7 Add the correct suffix: *-er*, *-ess*, *-ness*, or *-ism* to the words in bold and complete the sentences. You may have to change the spelling.

Your idea is stupid and crazy. Complete *madness*! **mad**

1 She's a very good _____ . She took some pictures of my party. **photograph**
2 I asked the _____ to bring us the check half an hour ago, and I haven't seen her since then! **waiter**
3 A female adult lion is called a _____ . **lion**
4 _____ is a type of discrimination, usually against women. **sex**
5 When Princess Diana died in 1997 there was a feeling of _____ in the UK. **sad**

Puzzle!

Complete the puzzle.

Across
2 The opposite of *tidy*.
5 The opposite of *moral*.
7 A person who has a farm is called a _____ .
8 The opposite of *useful*.

Down
1 A person who believes in racism is a _____ .
3 The opposite of *agree*.
4 If you are full of hope, you are _____ .
6 A female actor is an _____ .

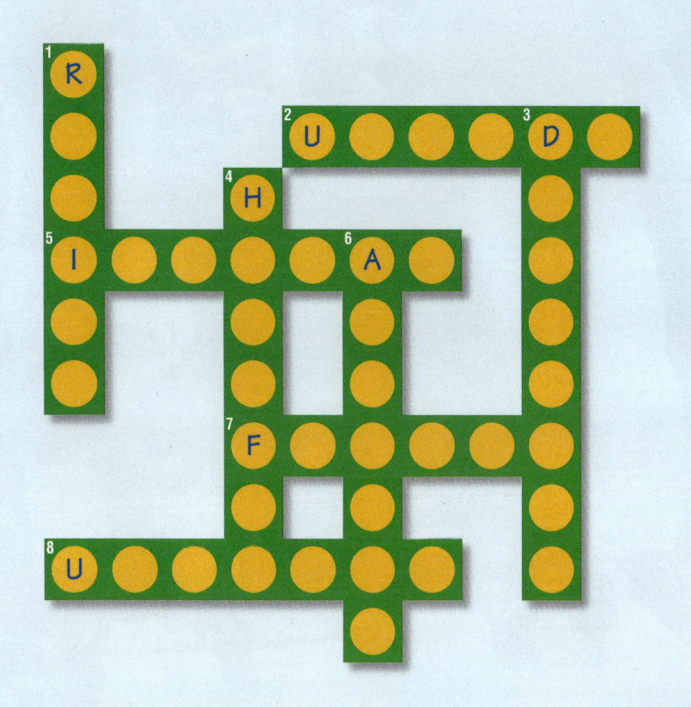

9 In-line skating in the park.

It's Sunday morning. The five friends meet in the park, to go in-line skating.

Jet Great news! Someone from Drama School e-mailed me. I have a scholarship interview tomorrow!
Bella Oh, tomorrow? That's good news.
Meg Have you told your dad?
Jet That's the bad news! No, I haven't told him. In fact, no one at home knows anything. But I think Dad suspects something.
Tom When he knows, I'm sure he'll be happy for you.
Jet I'm not so sure. Yesterday, he said that he wanted me to go to medical school! He wants me to be a doctor.
Bud Did you tell him that you didn't want to be a doctor?
Jet Sure. I said "no way!" I told him that I hated the sight of blood!
All Gross!
Meg Oh! Yuck!

Later, they stop for something to eat.

Tom Where will you go next year, Bella? Will you stay in New York?
Bella Oh, I don't know. What about you?
Tom I want to go to college. But Mom says she doesn't want me to go, because it's expensive.
Bella What does your dad say?
Tom He thinks college is a good idea.
Bud I told my parents that I didn't want to go to college next year. I said I wanted to go to Europe instead.
Meg Europe?
Bud Yes, to England. London maybe.
Meg Oh, I'll be back home in London then.
Bella Yeah, Meg. He knows that!
Bella, Jet, Tom Ooooooooooo!

Comprehension

1 Answer the questions.

When is Jet's scholarship interview?
Tomorrow
1. What does Jet's dad want him to be?
2. Does Jet agree with his dad?
3. Tom's mom doesn't want him to go to college. Why not?
4. What does Tom's dad think?
5. Where does Bud want to go next year?

What's your opinion?
Should Jet tell his dad about the interview?
Why? / Why not?

2 Who says these expressions?

Great news! *Jet*
1. Oh! Yuck! _____
2. What about you? _____
3. I'll be back home _____

How do you say these expressions in your language?

Communication

Good news, bad news!

3 Listen and repeat. Then, practice with a partner. Give the good news and the bad news!

Boy Good news!
Girl What is it?
Boy I got the job!

Girl Bad news!
Boy What is it?
Girl My test scores are terrible!

get / the job
pass / my driver's test
win / a prize
go / on vacation

test scores / terrible
lose / all my money
break / my leg
can't come / with you

You choose!

Reporting opinions

4 Listen and repeat. Then, ask and answer with a partner. Use the Communication box to help you.

Girl What does your dad say about college?
Boy He says that a college education is very important.

Boy What does your mom think about motorcycles?
Girl She thinks they're great!

Communication	
What do / does ...	*think / say about ... ?*
your parents	late night parties
most teenagers	learning English
your friend	girls who play soccer
your teacher	boys who learn ballet

Pronunciation

Stress and rhythm

5 Listen and underline the stressed words.

The sounds of poetry

6 Listen and repeat. Practice reading the poem aloud.

How <u>doth</u>[1] the little <u>crocodile</u>
<u>Improve</u> his shining <u>tail</u>,
And pour the waters of the Nile
On every golden scale!

How cheerfully he seems to grin
How neatly spreads his claws,
And welcomes little fishes in,
With gently smiling jaws!

Lewis Carroll (1832–1898)

1 = old word for does

Grammar

Reported speech: with reporting verbs in the present

1 First, study the examples. Then, complete the rule with the correct verbs from the examples.

Direct speech
"Hi! I'm Kate, Dave's girlfriend. I **like** Dave's hair!"
Reported speech
Kate **says** that she **likes** Dave's hair.

Direct speech
"Hello. We're Dave's parents. We **don't like** Dave's hair!"
Reported speech
Dave's parents say they **don't like** Dave's hair.

rule
If the verbs in direct speech are in the present (*like, don't like*)
and the reporting verb is in the present, (*says/say*)
then the verbs in reported speech are also in the present.
Kate **says** that she _____
Dave's parents **say** they _____

In reported speech, *that* is optional.

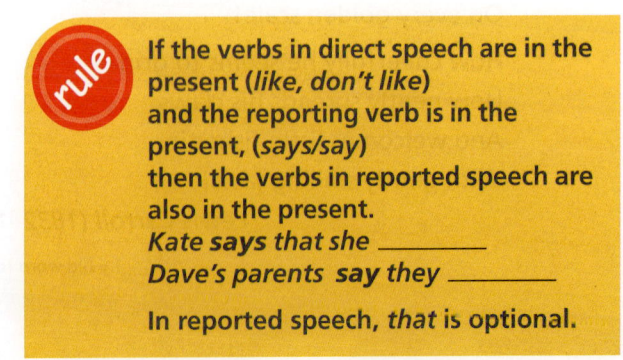

2 Change the direct speech into reported speech. Use *say/says* for the reporting verb.

Dave's sister: "I hate carrots."
Dave's sister *says* that she hates carrots.

1 Kate's mom: "I like Kate's new CD."
2 Dave's dad: "My wife doesn't like cooking."
3 Kate and Dave: "Our soccer team is the best."
4 Kate and her friend: "We don't have class on Saturdays."
5 Kate: "I can't go out tonight."
6 Kate's brother: "My French teacher is really cool."

LEARN THIS!

In reported speech, we change pronouns and possessive adjectives.
Kate: "**I'm** going."
→ Kate says that **she's** going.
Dave: "**My** shoes are wet."
→ Dave says **his** shoes are wet.
Dave's parents: "**We're** going."
→ Dave's parents say that **they're** going.
Kate's friends:
→ "**Our** shoes are wet."
Kate's friends say **their** shoes are wet.

3 What does your mom, or dad, or your friend often say to you?

You have to go to bed at ten o'clock.

My dad says I have to go to bed at ten!

Reported speech: with reporting verbs in the past

4 First, study the examples. Then, complete the rule with the correct verbs.

Dave, Kate's boyfriend:
"I **don't like** Kate's uniform!"
Dave **said** he **didn't like** Kate's uniform.

Kate's parents:
"We **like** Kate's uniform!"
Kate's parents **said** that they **liked** Kate's uniform.

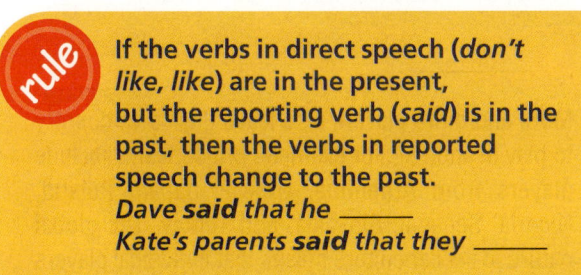

> **rule**
> If the verbs in direct speech (*don't like, like*) are in the present, but the reporting verb (*said*) is in the past, then the verbs in reported speech change to the past.
> Dave **said** that he _____
> Kate's parents **said** that they _____

5 Change the direct speech into reported speech. Use *said* for the reporting verb.

Kate and Dave: "Our friends like dancing."
Kate and Dave *said* that their friends *liked* dancing.

1 Dave's brother: "I'm an engineer."
2 Kate: "My father doesn't like the music."
3 Kate and Dave: "We often go to parties."
4 Dave: "My dad is a great cook."
5 Kate's sister: "I often buy new clothes."

Indefinite pronouns

6 First, practice the dialog with a partner. Then, complete the rules below. Use negative, affirmative, question forms.

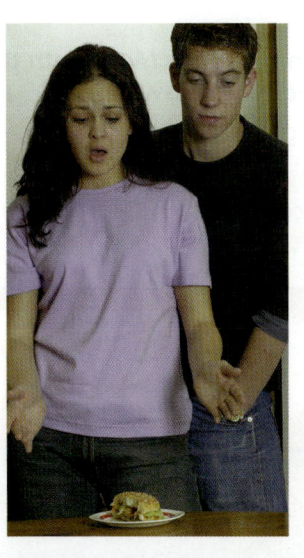

Carmen	**Someone** has eaten my hamburger!
Eddie	But there isn't **anyone** here!
Carmen	Listen! Is there **anyone** upstairs?
Eddie	Is there **anything** inside?
Carmen	No, there isn't **anything**!
Eddie	Yes, there is. There's **something** here.

> **rules**
> We use *someone* and *something* in _____ sentences.
> We use *anyone* and *anything* in _____ and _____ sentences.

7 Choose the correct indefinite pronouns.

We didn't buy *something* / (*anything*).
He saw (*someone*) / *anyone* he knew.
1 *Someone* / *Anyone* called you earlier.
2 Did you see *something* / *anything*?
3 *Something* / *Anything* strange happened last night.
4 Is *someone* / *anyone* listening to me?
5 I'm hungry. I haven't eaten *something* / *anything* today.

LEARN THIS!
We can also say **no one** and **nothing**.
No one in my family has a pet snake.
Nothing scares me – except snakes!

GRAMMAR HELP! page 89

10 The world of sports.

Reading

1 Read the text. Match the topics (A–D) with the paragraphs (1–4). Then, listen and check your answers.

A Soccer players as global superstars
B A golden prize
C The origins of soccer
D An International market

SOCCER A GLOBAL CULTURE

2 _____

Almost every country in the world competes for the World Cup. The first World Cup tournament took place in 1930. The tournament has taken place every four years since then, except for 1942 and 1946. The present cup was designed by an Italian, Silvio Gazzaniga. It is 1ft, 2 inches high, weighs 11lbs, and is made of solid gold.

3 _____

Successful coaches and managers move around the world as countries try to create the best possible team to win the World Cup. The Greek national team has had a German manager, and in the year 2000 the English national team appointed its first foreign coach, Sven Goren Eriksson, from Sweden.

1 _____

From its beginnings nearly five thousand years ago in China, soccer has grown into the most popular sport in the world. Versions of soccer were played in pre-Roman times. From the sixth century onwards different types of soccer were played in Colombia, France, Italy, and Britain. It was in Britain that soccer developed into the sport we know today.

4 _____

More and more players also leave their own country to play in another. For example, British teams include players from Argentina, Greece, Japan, Poland, Nigeria, Senegal, Slovakia, and Turkey. The global nature of soccer culture means that individual players can become world-famous superstars.

2 Find words or phrases in the text with these meanings.

origins (line 1)
beginnings

1 almost (line 1)
2 varieties (line 3)
3 contest (line 9)
4 but not in (line 11)
5 chose (line 19)
6 from a different country (line 19)
7 move away from (line 21)
8 single (line 25)

Discussion

3 What's your opinion?

Do you think that having foreign players is a good idea?

Why do you think soccer players leave their home country to play abroad?

Do you think players and coaches should stay in their own countries?

10

Vocabulary

New sports! Dangerous sports!

1 Read the text from the *Encyclopedia of Sports*. Match the sports (1–9) with the pictures (a–i). Then, listen and repeat, and check your answers.

ENCYCLOPEDIA OF SPORTS

Traditional sports such as soccer and tennis are very popular, but in recent years, a lot of people are trying newer sports such as in-line skating and **(1) skateboarding**.

However, some "new" sports, **(2) kick-boxing**, for example, are based on the ancient martial arts of China and Japan. Other new sports really are new! They include **(3) scuba-diving**, **(4) jet-skiing**, and **(5) snowboarding**, which is an exciting new winter sport.

For some new sports, such as **(6) sky-diving** and **(7) hang-gliding**, you need a good head for heights!

Some new sports are dangerous, for example **(8) abseiling**, where you come down a rock face very quickly. One of the most popular new sports is **(9) bungee jumping**, where you tie a long piece of elastic to your feet, and jump off something very high, for example a bridge or a crane! Don't try it without expert help!

Sports	Pictures
1 skateboarding	= (g)
2 kick-boxing	____

2 Listen to the teenagers. Complete the chart. Which sports in exercise 1 have they tried? Which sports would they like to try?

	has tried	would like to try
1 Marcos, 17 from Brazil	scuba-diving	____
2 Rachel, 16 from the USA	____	____
3 Yoko, 15, from Japan	____	____
4 Don, 16, from Canada	____	____

3 Use the Conversation Guide to ask and answer about the sports in exercise 1.

Have you tried any new or dangerous sports?

Yes, I've tried … / No, I haven't.

Did you like it? / Would you like to try one?

Yes, I did. / Yes I would.

No, I didn't. / No I wouldn't.

Why?/Why not? / Because …

WORD LIST page 94

10 Writing — Connecting ideas

Writing about special people

1 First, read the model composition. Then, discuss how you say the connectors in your language.

MODEL COMPOSITION

The person I admire most
Introduction

The person I admire most is Christopher Reeve. I have seen a lot of his movies **and** a television documentary about him. He is most famous for the Superman movies **although** he also acted in over thirty other movies.

Main part

Reeve wanted an education; he **also** wanted to act. After graduating, Reeve went to Cornell University. **However**, he worked as a professional actor at the same time. In 1995 he had a horse riding accident. He was paralyzed, **yet** continued to work. He fought to improve his condition, **in addition**, he created the U.S.'s first center to teach paralyzed people to live more independently.

Conclusion

Christopher Reeve is the person I admire the most **because** he is an inspiration to people with disabilities. He was a Hollywood star **but** also very human. Sadly he died in 2004.

2 Complete the chart with the connectors in the composition.

Connecting similar ideas	Connecting contrasting ideas
and	although
___	___
___	___
___	___

tip! Use connectors to link *similar* ideas, and *contrasting* ideas.

3 Circle the correct connector.

He was very rich, or / (although) he wasn't very generous. (= *contrasting ideas*)

Her fans adore her (and) / yet they send letters from all over the world. (= *similar ideas*)

1 He is a computer genius, *but / and* he is very successful.
2 She was popular with ordinary people, *but / and* politicians did not like her.
3 He was terrible at school; *also / however*, at college he was a top student in his year.
4 She usually finishes her concerts with her latest hits *or / because* they are the most popular.
5 He is very successful, very famous, and very rich, *and / yet* he is not proud or vain.
6 She sometimes works for the United Nations, *in addition / although*, she dedicates her performances to the UN.

Your writing task

4 Write a composition about a special person. Use connectors to link similar ideas, or contrasting ideas. Use the connectors on this page, and these ideas to help you.

The person I admire most.
The person I would most like to meet.
The person who changed my life.
The person I would most like to be.

COMMUNICATION ACTIVITY 5
Student A turn to page 74   Student B turn to page 77

10

Song — Sisters are Doin' it for Themselves

1 Listen and complete the song. Use the words in the box.

> celebrate change kitchen man
> say state ~~time~~ too true
> woman you you

2 How many times do the pronouns *we* and *you* appear? Who or what do they refer to?

3 How do you say *Standing on their own two feet* in your language?

Sisters are Doin' it for Themselves

Now there was a **time**
When they used to (1) _____
That behind every great (2) _____
There had to be a great (3) _____

But in these times of (4) _____
You know that it's no longer (5) _____ .
So we're comin' out of the (6) _____
'Cause there's somethin' we forgot to say to (7) _____

We say: Sisters are doin' it for themselves.
Standin' on their own two feet.
And ringin' on their own bells.
Sisters are doin' it for themselves.

Now this is a song to (8) _____
The conscious liberation of the female (9) _____
Mothers – daughters and their daughters (10) _____
Woman to woman we're singin' with (11) _____

PROGRESS REVIEW: UNITS 9 and 10

	Difficult ☹	OK 😐	Easy! ☺
Communication			
• good news!	☐	☐	☐
• bad news!	☐	☐	☐
• reporting opinions (She says, he thinks)	☐	☐	☐
Grammar			
• reported speech (They say that …)	☐	☐	☐
• with reporting verbs in the present	☐	☐	☐
• with reporting verbs in the past	☐	☐	☐
Vocabulary			
• new sports! dangerous sports!	☐	☐	☐

11 Graduation day.

It's graduation day. Bella and Bud have to give a "thank you" speech.

Tom Whose cap is this? Is it yours Bella?
Bud No, it isn't hers. It's mine. This one's yours, Tom.
Bella I feel really nervous about the speech.
Bud Me, too. If you gave all the speech Bella, I'd feel better.
Bella Bud! Don't be such a coward!
Meg Let's rehearse.
Bella Good idea. *On behalf of all the graduating students, I would like to thank our teachers.*
Bud Then it's my turn. *We are grateful for all your classes. And thanks for all those tests and exams! We will never forget Lincoln High!*
Tom Hey! Terrific!
Meg Well done!

After the ceremony, and the speeches.

Tom I feel kind of sad. I'm going to miss all my friends.
Bella I feel excited! I'm going to study biology, in California.
Tom But if you stayed in New York, you'd still see Jet.
Bella Oh, Jet and me . . . . We're just good friends now. That's cool.
Meg If I lived in California, I'd go surfing all the time!

In the evening, the students celebrate with their parents.

Jet Hi, everyone!
Tom Jet! Congratulations on the scholarship. Oh! Your dad – sorry, I, forgot!
Jet's dad No problem. Everything's fine. If Antonio went to medical school, he wouldn't be happy. I'm proud of him.
Jet So! Vacation time!
Bud Yeah. Meg and I are going to London.
Meg It's been great here in America. But I want to go home now!
Jet's dad Good luck to all of you. Cheers! Here's to you!
All To us!

Comprehension

1 Choose the best word to describe the characters' feelings and emotions. Use your dictionary to help you, if necessary.

Bella and Bud feel confident / *anxious* about their speech.

1. Tom feels *unhappy / happy* about going away to college.
2. Bella feels *excited / sad* about going to California.
3. Bella feels *OK / sad* about her and Jet.
4. Mr. Gonzalez feels *proud / angry* about Jet's scholarship.

What's your opinion?

Why does Tom say, "Your dad – sorry, I forgot!"

2 Who says these expressions?

Don't be such a coward! *Bella*

1. Well done! _____
2. I feel kind of sad. _____
3. Cheers! Here's to you! _____

How do you say these expressions in your language?

Communication

Well-wishing

3 Listen and repeat. Then, practice with a partner. Match the statements (1–5) with the wishes (a–e).

Boy It's my birthday today!
Girl Happy Birthday!

Girl I've just won a scholarship!
Boy Congratulations!

1. I'm taking a test tomorrow.
2. It's my birthday.
3. I have flu.
4. I've passed!
5. See you when I get back.

a) Get well soon!
b) Good luck!
c) Many happy returns!
d) Safe journey!
e) Well done!

Thanks!

4 Listen and repeat. Then, practice with a partner. Use the Communication box to help you.

On behalf of all the students, we wish to thank …

And we would also like to thank …

Communication

Useful "thank you" expressions
We want to say thanks to …
We would like to say thank you for …
We wish to thank X for…
Special thanks to …

Pronunciation

Intonation

5 Listen to the poem. Notice when the intonation goes up [↗] and down [↘].

The sounds of poetry

6 Listen and repeat. Practice reading the poem aloud.

Little Fly,
Thy summer's play
My thoughtless hand
Has brush'd away.

Am not I
A fly like [1]thee?
Or art not [2]thou
A man like me?

For I dance,
And drink, and sing,
Till some blind hand
Shall brush my wing.

If thought is life
And strength and breath,
And the want
Of thought is death;

Then am I
A happy fly,
If I live
Or if I die.

William Blake (1757–1827)

[1] thee = you in old English
[2] thou = you in old English

11

Grammar

Second conditional

1 Study the examples. Then, answer the questions (1–4) about the meaning of the second conditional.

If Eddie **had** a lot of money, he **would go/'d go** on a world cruise.

1 Does Eddie have a lot of money?
2 Will he go on a world cruise? Why?/Why not?

If Carmen **didn't practice** every day, she **would not improve**.

3 Does Carmen practice every day?
4 Will she improve? Why?/Why not?

2 Look the examples in exercise 1 again. Answer the questions about the formation of the second conditional.

1 Which tense do we use in the *If* clause?
2 What do we use in the main clause?

3 Complete the *If* clauses in the sentences. Use the simple past (affirmative or negative) of the verbs in parentheses.

If I (**go**) to the gym every day, I'd have really big muscles.

If I went to the gym every day, I'd have really big muscles.

1 If I (**have**) a lot of money, I'd buy a private jet.
2 If my brother (**not watch**) TV so much, he would have more time to study.
3 If our school (**be**) in England, I wouldn't need an English pen pal.
4 If you (**not stay**) out so late, you wouldn't be so tired!

4 Complete the main clauses in the sentences. Use *'d* or *wouldn't*.

If Martine won a lot of money, she (**buy**) a lot of diamonds.

If Martine won a lot of money, she 'd buy a lot of diamonds.

1 If you asked her to dance, she (**be**) really happy.
2 If you didn't talk in class, you (**learn**) a lot more!
3 If he lived at my house, my dad (**not let**) him play his guitar.
4 We (**not get**) good jobs if we didn't study English.

5 Complete the sentences about you, your friends, and your family. Use the second conditional.

If we were very rich we wouldn't buy a big car. We 'd buy a luxury yacht!

1 If I had a pen pal in the USA, ____ .
2 If my best friend moved to Canada, ____ .
3 If my family didn't live in this town, ____ .
4 If our teachers didn't give us so much homework, ____ .
5 If ____ .

You choose!

LEARN THIS!

We use the **first conditional** to express things that possibly **will** happen.
If I pass my test, I'll be really happy!
We use the **second conditional** to express things that probably **will not** happen.
If I won the lottery, I'd be really rich!

Possessive pronouns

6 Complete the chart. Use the words in the box. Then check your answers with the table on p90.

> ~~mine~~ ~~yours~~ ours hers theirs his yours its

Possessive adjectives	Possessive pronouns
my	mine
your	yours
her	(1) _____
his	(2) _____
its	(3) _____
our	(4) _____
your	(5) _____
their	(6) _____

7 Complete the dialog with the correct possessive pronouns.

The sunglasses are Martine's. They're hers.

1 The baseball cap belongs to me. It's _____ .
2 This towel is Oscar's. It's _____ .
3 I don't have a camera, so my sister lent me _____ .
4 Does the umbrella belong to you, Oscar? Is it _____ ?
5 The beach ball doesn't belong to us. It isn't _____ .
6 Those children were playing with a ball, so it's probably _____ .

LEARN THIS!

Using **Whose ...?**
Whose is this baseball cap?   It's Kim's.
Whose towel is this?   It's mine!

GRAMMAR HELP!   page 90

Study skills

How do you study for tests?

8 Complete the questionnaire. Compare your score with your friends' score.

Study Quiz   YES NO

Before tests
Do you ...
1 start to study a few days before? ☐ ☐
2 study a little bit each day? ☐ ☐
3 check your frequent mistakes? ☐ ☐
4 use the grammar help in this book? ☐ ☐
5 memorize useful vocabulary? ☐ ☐
6 test yourself and a friend? ☐ ☐
7 try to get a good night's sleep? ☐ ☐

During tests
Do you ...
8 read the questions carefully? ☐ ☐
9 plan the time you need for each question? ☐ ☐
10 leave time to check your answers? ☐ ☐

TOTAL "YES" ANSWERS

KEY
Score 1 for each "Yes" answer. Score 0 for each "No" answer.
0–3 Careful! You need to improve.
4–7 OK! But there is room for improvement.
8–10 Congratulations! You're probably very good at tests and examinations.

12 Varieties of English.

Reading

1 Read the text and complete it with the words in the box. Then, listen and check your answers.

> article   difficulty   For   form   including   ~~mean~~   often
> People   professions   short   way

COMMUNICATING IN English

English is the most widely-spoken language in the world. But that doesn't mean that all English speakers can understand each other! **(1)** _____ speak different varieties of English according to their nationality, region, profession – and even the form of communication they are using.

NATIONAL VARIETIES

There are several national varieties of English, and native English speakers from different countries sometimes have **(2)** _____ communicating. If you asked for chips in the UK, you would get French fries. In Australia, a hotel is **(3)** _____ just a pub. And in South Africa, a robot is a stop signal!

ENGLISH FOR SPECIAL PURPOSES

Then there are the special types of English for different jobs and **(4)** _____ . Scientists, lawyers, and doctors can often only be understood by other scientists, lawyers, and doctors! If you opened a medical journal and found an **(5)** _____ called *Idiopathic intracranial hypertension*, would you know what it was about?

ENGLISH AND TECHNOLOGY

Technology has changed the **(6)** _____ we use English. In e-mail, many people do not use punctuation or capital letters. An extreme example of this is found in text messaging – a kind of mini e-mail for cell phones. Because the screen on a phone is so small, the messages have to be **(7)** _____ . So people use abbreviations. **(8)** _____ example, this symbol: @, means *at*, B4 means *before*, GR8 means *great*, and XLNT means *excellent*.

INTERNATIONAL ENGLISH

But the **(9)** _____ of English spoken and understood by the most people in the world is "international English". English as an International Language (EIL) is spoken by millions of people around the world, **(10)** _____ all the people who are learning English as a foreign language. And that includes you!

2 Listen to the students. Complete the chart. Which variety of English will they be interested in?

- **A** Doi
- **B** Beatrice
- **C** Carlo
- **D** Dona

	A	B	C	D
Medical English	○	○	○	○
Scientific English	✓	○	○	○
Text messaging	○	○	○	○
American English	○	○	○	○

3 Look at the text message below. How would we write it in standard English?

> CU @ 9 2NITE. DON'T B L8!

Vocabulary

Word families

1 Complete the chart of word families. Use your dictionary if necessary!

WORD FAMILIES

	noun	verb	adjective	adverb
	actor	to act	✕	✕
1	arrival	_____	✕	✕
2	_____	to discuss	✕	✕
	happiness	✕	happy	happily
3	_____	✕	honest	honestly
4	politeness	✕	polite	_____
5	possibility	✕	_____	possibly
6	help	to help	helpful/helpless	helpfully/_____
7	hope	to hope	hopeful/hopeless	hopefully/_____
8	origin	to originate	original	_____

2 Choose one word family from each group. Write sentences to illustrate the meanings of each family member. Write the first one below.

Tom Hanks is my favorite **actor**.

If you want to learn how **to act**, you have to go to drama school.

3 Identify the correct part of speech for each word (1–4). Use your dictionary to check your answers. Then, write the words in the chart below.

1 to argue — verb
2 confidence — _____
3 fortunately — _____
4 useful — _____

	noun	verb	adjective	adverb
1	argument	to argue	✕	✕
2	_____	✕	_____	_____
3	_____	✕	_____	_____
4	_____	_____	_____	_____

4 Use your dictionary to help you find the other members of each word family.

WORD LIST — page 94

12 Writing — Sequencing events

Writing about special occasions

1 First, read the model composition. Then, discuss how you say the sequencing words in your language.

MODEL COMPOSITION

The best weekend of my life

My name is Laura and I live in Denver, Colorado. The best weekend of my life was three months ago. My mom and dad took me to *Universal Studios* in Hollywood! We flew to LA on Friday May 5.

The next day was fantastic! **First**, we did a general tour of the studios. **After** that, we went for a ride in *Jurassic Park*. We saw lots of dinosaurs. **Before** lunch, we saw a fabulous parade, with bands. **Then** for lunch I had a "Tangoburger" in *Café Tu Tu Tango*! **Next**, we went to the special effects studio. We saw how they create monsters, earthquakes, and spaceships. **Soon** it was 5 pm. I had a delicious ice-cream cone. **Later**, in the evening, we saw the new Tom Cruise movie. **Finally**, we watched a spectacular fireworks display.

On Sunday, before we flew home, we took a tour around Beverley Hills, where the movie stars live. I will remember that weekend all my life.

2 Arrange Laura's photos (A–D) in the correct order of what she did and ate.

order	1	2	3	4
picture	C	___	___	___

tip! When you are describing events, or narrating a story, use days, dates, times, and especially sequencing words to indicate the order of events.

3 Answer the questions about the sequence of events in Laura's weekend.

If Laura went to Hollywood three months ago, what month is it now? August.
1 On which day of the week did she visit *Universal Studios*?
2 What did she see before she ate lunch?
3 At what time did Laura eat an ice-cream cone?
4 Where did she go after lunch?
5 What was the last thing Laura did on Saturday?
6 How many nights did she spend in LA?
7 What was the date of her flight home to Denver?

Your writing task

4 Write a composition about a special occasion. Use dates, days, times, and sequencing words to describe the events. Use the sequencing words in exercise 1 and these ideas to help you.

The best weekend of my life
A family celebration
My first visit to a big city
The day I met my boyfriend/girlfriend

COMMUNICATION ACTIVITY 6
Student A turn to page 74   Student B turn to page 77

Song — Money, Money, Money!

1. Listen and put the lines of the chorus (a–i) in their correct order (1–9).

2. Find two examples of the second conditional in the song. Explain their meanings.

3. How do you say these words in your language?
   - bills
   - fortune
   - rich
   - wealthy

   What is the connection between them?

Money, Money, Money

I work all night, I work all day
To pay the bills I have to pay – ain't it sad!
And still there never seems to be
A single penny left for me – that's too bad!
In my dreams I have a plan:
If I got me a wealthy man,
I wouldn't have to work at all,
I'd fool around and have a ball.

a) In the rich man's world.   ___
b) Must be funny,   ___
c) If I had a little money,   ___
d) In the rich man's world.   ___
e) Always sunny,   ___
f) It's a rich man's world.   ___
g) Money, money, money,   1
h) Aha, all the things I could do! ___
i) Money, money, money,   ___

A man like that is hard to find,
But I can't get him off my mind – ain't it sad!
And if he happens to be free,
I bet he wouldn't fancy me – that's too bad!
So, I must leave, I'll have to go
To Las Vegas or Monaco,
And win a fortune in a game –
My life will never be the same

PROGRESS REVIEW: UNITS 11 and 12

	Difficult ☹	OK 😐	Easy! ☺
Communication			
• well-wishing *(Congratulations)*	☐	☐	☐
• thanks *(On behalf of all …)*	☐	☐	☐
Grammar			
• second conditional *(If I had …, I'd …)*	☐	☐	☐
• possessive pronouns *(mine, yours, theirs)*	☐	☐	☐
Vocabulary			
• word families *(help, to help, helpful, helplessly)*	☐	☐	☐

Review: Units 9 to 12

Grammar

Reported speech: with reporting verbs in the present

1 Change the direct speech into reported speech. Use *say/says* as the reporting verb.

- I love rap music. — Tony
- 1 I go to lots of rock concerts. — Katrin
- 2 My hobby is skateboarding.
- 3 I love playing my CDs really loudly.
- 4 We don't like rap or rock music. — Sue / Ken
- 5 Our favorite type of music is classical.

Tony says *he loves rap music*.
1 Katrin says _____ .
2 Tony _____ .
3 Katrin _____ .
4 Sue and Ken _____ .
5 Sue and Ken _____ .

Reported speech: with reporting verbs in the past

2 Change the direct speech in exercise 1 to reported speech. This time, use *said* as the reporting verb.

Tony *said* he *loved* rap music.

Indefinite pronouns

3 Complete the sentences with *something, someone, anything,* or *anyone*.

Hello? Is there *anyone* at home?
1 Be quiet! I think I can hear _____ talking outside.
2 It is very dark in here. I can't see _____ .
3 There's _____ wrong with my computer.
4 I don't know _____ who doesn't like music.

Second conditional

4 Choose the correct verb.

If we went up the tower, we*'ll have / 'd have* a good view.
If we went up the tower, we *'d have* a good view.

1 If he was rich, he *bought / would buy* that sports car.
2 If she *didn't study / wouldn't study* so hard, she wouldn't do very well at school.
3 If she *liked / would like* him, she'd dance with him.
4 If the wall wasn't so high, they*'d be able / were able* to climb over it.

Possessive pronouns

5 Complete the sentences. Use *mine, yours, his, hers, ours,* or *theirs*.

This bag belongs to me. It's *mine*.
1 These people own this house. It's _____ .
2 Is this your skateboard? Is it _____ ?
3 I think the bag belongs to that girl. I'm sure it's _____ .
4 We own this island and everything on it. It's all _____ .
5 That looks like my brother's car. Yes, it's definitely _____ .

64

Vocabulary

New sports! Dangerous sports!

6 Name the sports and match them with the pictures.

	Picture
bacus-vigdin scuba-diving	C
1 yks-nigvid _____	_____
2 tej-ginkis _____	_____
3 nebuge pigmunj _____	_____
4 gahn-digglin _____	_____
5 snakebirdgoat _____	_____
6 genialsib _____	_____
7 ikkc-bignox _____	_____
8 dobsonginwar _____	_____

Word families

7 Identify the correct part of speech: *adjective*, *adverb*, *noun*, or *verb*, for the words in bold.

My girlfriend and I don't like to **argue**.   *verb*

1 But we nearly had a big **argument** last night. _____
2 She said that I wasn't **helpful** around the house. _____
3 I said that I would **happily** help her if she asked. _____
4 She **laughed**, and told me I was lazy. _____
5 **Fortunately**, someone rang the doorbell then. _____
6 We decided to **discuss** the subject another time. _____
7 It isn't **polite** to fight in front of friends. _____
8 I'm not looking forward to our next **discussion**. _____

8 Complete the sentences with the correct form of the word in bold.

I'm very *hopeful* about these tests. I think everyone will do well. (**hope**)

1 There is a ____ that I won't be able to come to the party next week. (**possible**)
2 I have never seen such a ____ baby before in my life! (**happiness**)
3 She still doesn't know how to ____ her cell phone. (**useful**)
4 The young politician spoke ____ in front of the TV cameras. (**confidence**)
5 We could hear the sound of ____ coming from the class next door. (**laugh**)

Puzzle!

Complete the puzzle with sports from Exercise 6. One sport does not fit!

The missing sport is _____-_____

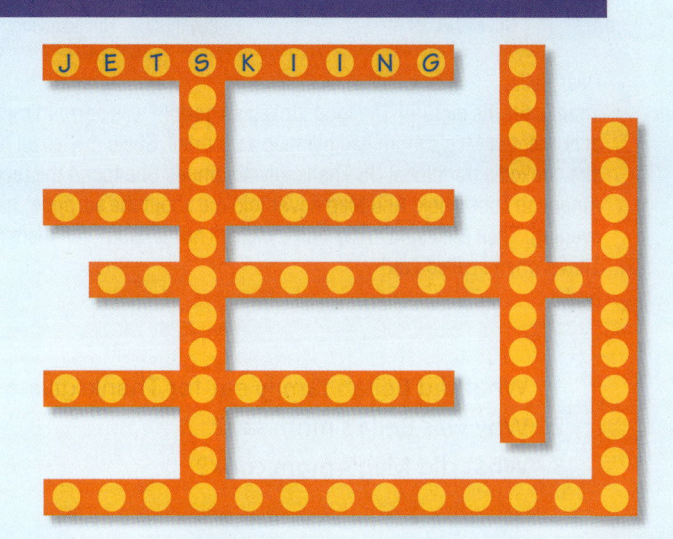

J E T S K I I N G

Bonus unit 1

An American tradition: Thanksgiving

1 Bud is visiting Meg in London. Read Bella and Bud's e-mails and answer the questions below.

FROM:	bella@girltalk.now.usa	TO:	bud@london.online.co.uk
DATE:	November 22	SUBJECT:	Thanksgiving

Dear Bud,
I hope you like the photo of our Thanksgiving dinner! It was a very traditional meal. The turkey came from Uncle Joe's farm, and Aunt Betty made the cranberry sauce. Mom cooked sweet potatoes the way you like, and earlier, she had made my favorite – pumpkin pie. Before we started to eat, Mom had become a bit sad. She wanted the whole family to be together for Thanksgiving, as usual. She misses you a lot! I had decided to e-mail the picture to you – and then you called us. Mom felt much happier when she'd heard your voice. Your call was just what Mom had wanted. You chose the right time to call. Well done!
Bella

FROM:	bud@london.online.co.uk.	TO:	bella@girltalk.now.usa
DATE:	November 23	SUBJECT:	Thanksgiving

Dear Bella,
Thanks for the picture! The food looked so good! I was sorry to miss Thanksgiving at home, but Meg's mom had planned a surprise. She'd invited all her family, and she cooked a traditional US Thanksgiving dinner. She found the recipes in an American cook book. And Meg never told me about the surprise! It was a great evening. Then Meg said "Why don't you call home, Bud? Tell them all about it." That's when I called you!
Bud

1 What did Bella's family eat for Thanksgiving dinner?
2 Why was Bella's mom sad?
3 What did Meg's mom cook?

2 Study the pairs of sentences. In each pair, circle the event that happened first.

a) Bella's mom cooked sweet potatoes.
(b)) Mom made a pumpkin pie.

1 a) Bella's family started to eat.
   b) Mom became a bit sad.

2 a) Bella decided to e-mail the picture.
   b) Bud called his family.

3 a) Mom felt much happier.
   b) Mom heard Bud's voice.

4 a) Mom wanted Bud to call.
   b) Bud chose the right time to call.

5 a) Meg's mom invited all her family.
   b) She cooked a traditional American Thanksgiving dinner.

Past perfect

3 Study the examples and complete the rule.

Billy ate the ice cream at ten o'clock.

Jenny didn't have any ice cream.
Jenny didn't have any ice cream, because Billy had eaten it all.

Oscar went for a swim at two o'clock.

Oscar fell asleep on the beach at four o'clock.
Oscar fell asleep on the beach after he'd been for a swim.

rule   We form the past perfect with _____ + the _____ of the main verb.

BONUS POINT!

We use the **past perfect** to describe a past action that happened *before* another event in the past.

Note: we use *had / hadn't* with all pronouns.

4 Complete the sentences. Use the past perfect.

When the police arrived at the National Gallery they found… .
Thieves (stole) many works of art.
Thieves *had stolen* many works of art.
1 They (take) a valuable painting.
2 They (broke) a beautiful vase.
3 The museum guards (not hear) any noise.
4 They (not see) the thieves.

The reporting verbs *say* and *tell*

BONUS POINT!

We use *say* when there is *no* personal object.
He **said** that he was coming.

We use *tell* when there is a personal object.
They **told us** that they weren't coming.

Note: *that* is always optional.

5 Complete the sentences. Use *say (said)* or *tell (told)*.

She *told* us that the plane was leaving.
The pilot *said* the plane was leaving.
1 Mom _____ dad that she was really pleased with her present.
2 They _____ they were not arriving until 11 pm.
3 He _____ that he was going to the USA.
4 Our teacher _____ us we had passed the test!

GRAMMAR HELP!   page 91

Bonus unit 2

A British tradition: Wimbledon

1 First, read Bud's e-mail, and choose five words which are new to you. Then, with a partner, guess the meanings. Don't use a dictionary!

FROM:	bud@london.online.co.uk	TO:	bella@girltalk.now.usa
DATE:	June 25	SUBJECT:	Wimbledon

Hi, sis!

Meg and I went to Wimbledon yesterday! It was fabulous. We couldn't afford tickets for reserved seats, because they are too expensive. But there are a few cheaper tickets on sale each day. The problem is – you have to wait in line for hours and hours!

So on Tuesday evening we joined the all-night line for tickets! We camped out through the night. We were warm enough because we had sleeping bags. At 7 am, Meg's mom brought us some breakfast, and she lent us her cell phone.

On Wednesday morning, we were lucky, and we got two tickets. They sold out really quickly. If we hadn't waited in line all night, we wouldn't have gotten any. And if we had waited in line on Monday night for Tuesday's games, we wouldn't have seen any tennis at all, because on Tuesday it rained all day!

We ate strawberries and cream. It's a famous Wimbledon tradition. But they are so expensive! We didn't have any money for the bus fare home. If Meg's mom hadn't lent us her cell phone, we would have had a very, very long walk! Fortunately, we called her dad on his cell phone. He came and drove us to Meg's house.

England has been great. But I'm looking forward to coming home next week in time for the Independence Day parade.

Bud x

2 Correct the false statements.

Bud and Meg bought **expensive** tickets.
Bud and Meg bought cheaper tickets

1. Bud and Meg had to wait in line all **day**.
2. Bud and Meg joined the line on **Wednesday** evening.
3. Meg's mom came to see them at **7 pm**.
4. Bud and Meg watched the games on **Thursday**.
5. Meg's **dad** lent them **his** phone.
6. Meg's **mom** took them home by car.

Third conditional

3 First, read the examples. Then, answer questions 1–4.

Oh, no! If we **had come** early, we **would have gotten** tickets!

1 Did they come early?
2 Did they get tickets?

Fantastic! If we **hadn't come** early, we **wouldn't have gotten** tickets!

3 Did they come early.
4 Did they get tickets?

4 Read the examples in Exercise 1 again. Pay special attention to the verbs. Then complete the rules for the third conditional.

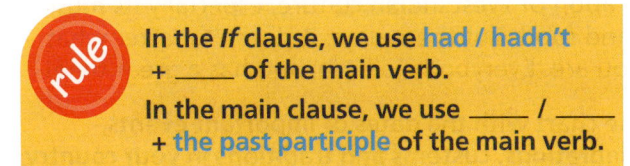

> **rule**
> In the *If* clause, we use **had / hadn't** + _____ of the main verb.
> In the main clause, we use _____ / _____ + the past participle of the main verb.

BONUS POINT!
You use the third conditional when you imagine a situation in the past which did *not* happen.

5 Complete the sentences. Use the correct forms of the missing verbs.

1 If he had run faster, he (won) the race.
2 If she hadn't studied every day, she (not pass) her English test. 
3 If she (wear) her coat, she wouldn't have been cold. 
4 If he (not score) two goals, his team would have lost. 

too and *enough*

6 Study the examples. What do you say to Martine? Use *too* or *enough*.

What do you think of my clothes?

hat / big — Your hat is *too* big!
belt / long — Your belt isn't long *enough*.

1 handbag / small
2 jacket / long
3 shoes / high
4 skirt / short
5 handbag / big
6 jacket / clean
7 shoes / comfortable
8 clothes / fashionable

GRAMMAR HELP! page 91

Bonus unit 3

Festivals, celebrations, customs, and traditions!

1 Take turns to ask and answer with different partners. The answers are in the chart on the next page!

1. In which month is Chinese New Year?
2. Which country celebrates Memorial Day?
3. When and where is Bonfire Night celebrated?
4. Who is the patron saint of Wales?
5. On which day and where is Labor Day celebrated?
6. Why is July 4 an important day in the USA?

Write four more questions for your partner!

1. _____
2. _____
3. _____
4. _____

2 Read and listen to the descriptions. Complete them with the name of the correct festival or celebration.

Oh, _____ is really great. Everybody sings traditional and patriotic songs. Some people wear green clothes and paint their faces green. In New York, they have an enormous parade. And people celebrate by drinking a lot of beer and whisky!

In Britain, we don't celebrate Mardi Gras, but we do have the _____ , which is now the biggest street carnival in Europe. It was originally a celebration of West Indian culture, especially its music, dance, costume, and food. But these days, it doesn't matter what race or religion you are. Everybody joins in, and has a great time!

3 Complete the chart with the dates of important events, festivals, celebrations, customs and traditions in your country. Write about one of them. Include information about

- the name of the event
- its date
- what it is about
- special customs and traditions
- special food, costumes, music, or dances

Month	International	The USA	The UK	Your country!
January	**New Year's Day** 1st	**The President's Inauguration Day** 20th - every 4 years **Martin Luther King Day** Third Monday		
February	*Yuan Tan* * Chinese New Year	**Valentine's Day** 14th **Presidents' Day** Third Monday **Mardi Gras** *	**Valentine's Day** 14th **Pancake Day** *	
March	**International Women's Day** 8th	**St Patrick's Day** 17th patron saint of Ireland	**St David's Day** 1st patron saint of Wales **St Patrick's Day** 17th patron saint of Ireland **Mother's Day** Fourth Sunday in Lent	
April		**Easter** *	**Easter** * **The Queen's official birthday** 21st **St George's Day** 23rd patron saint of England **Shakespeare's birthday** 23rd	
May	**International Labor Day** 1st	**Mother's Day** Second Sunday **Memorial Day** Fourth Monday	**The Cup Final** *	
June	**The World Cup** * every 4 years	**Father's Day** Third Sunday	**Father's Day** Third Sunday **Wimbledon fortnight** *	
July	**The Olympic Games** * every 4 years	**Independence Day** 4th		
August			**The Notting Hill Carnival** Last Saturday	
September		**Labor Day** First Monday		
October	**United Nations Day** 24th	**Columbus Day** 12th **Hallowe'en** 31st	**Hallowe'en** 31st	
November	*Diwali* * Hindu New Year	**Presidential elections** every 4 years* **Veterans' Day** 11th **Thanksgiving Day** Fourth Thursday	**Guy Fawkes Night** 5th Bonfire Night **Remembrance Day** 11th **St Andrew's Day** 30th patron saint of Scotland	
December	**New Year's Eve** 31st	**Christmas Day** 25th	**Christmas Day** 25th	

* The date isn't the same every year.

Communication activities

Communication activity 1

Student A

Two students have applied for the same job in a music store.

ARE YOU A STUDENT?
Would you like a SUMMER JOB?
DAVE'S MUSIC, is looking for 1 STORE CLERK for the summer vacation.
5 days a week, including some Saturdays.
Driver's license would be an advantage.
Apply to Dave Gibson <dave@gibson.co.uk>

1 Ask Student B about Sally, and complete the form below.

What's her full name?
How old is she?
Has she worked before? Where? When?
Has she passed her driver's test? When?
What are her hobbies and interests?

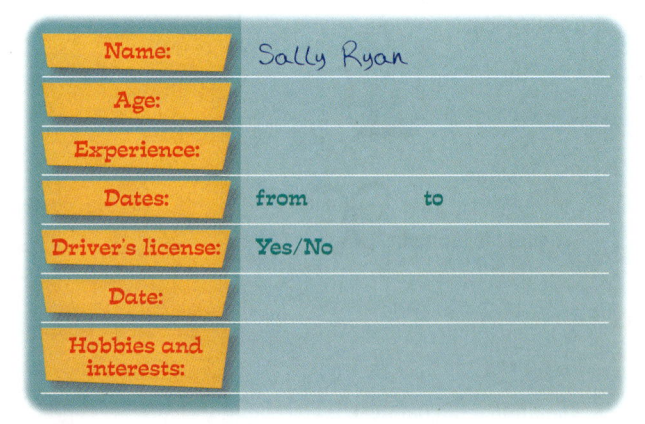

Name:	Sally Ryan
Age:	
Experience:	
Dates:	from to
Driver's license:	Yes/No
Date:	
Hobbies and interests:	

2 Read Alan's letter, and answer Student B's questions.

May 3 2002
Dear Mr. Gibson,
I am interested in working in your music store. I am seventeen years old, and I have worked in a store once before. That was my uncle's book store, and I worked there in June and July last summer. I enjoyed the work, but I am more interested in music than books. I play the guitar and spend lots of money on CDs. I passed my driver's test in February.
Yours Sincerely,
Alan Toper

3 Who do you think is the best candidate for the job? Why?

Communication activity 2

Student A

Anthony and Helen are doing a treasure hunt in New York. The first person to complete all the tasks on the list wins a prize.

1 Ask Student B what tasks Helen has completed so far, and fill in her sheet.
   Student A: Has Helen taken a photo of Times Square yet?
   Student B: Yes, she has.

The New York City Treasure Hunt

Name: Helen Barker

Tasks:
- take a photo of Times Square ☑
- get the autograph of a New York bus driver ☐
- travel on the subway ☐
- cross the Hudson River ☐
- feed the ducks in Central Park ☐
- buy something with "I ♥ New York" on it ☐
- get a photo taken with a police officer ☐

2 Now answer Student B's questions about Anthony.

The New York City Treasure Hunt

Name: Anthony Martin

Tasks:
- take a photo of Times Square ☑
- get the autograph of a New York bus driver ☐
- travel on the subway ☑
- cross the Hudson River ☑
- feed the ducks in Central Park ☑
- buy something with "I ♥ New York" on it ☐
- get a photo taken with a police officer ☑

3 Who do you think is going to win the treasure hunt?

Communication activity 3

Student A

1 Choose a job. Answer Student B's questions.

WILDLIFE PHOTOGRAPHER

I travel around the world.
I take photos of animals in their natural environment.
I often have to get up early in the morning and drive to where the animals are.
I need to use a special camera. Sometimes I send pictures to my editor via my computer.

NURSE

I work in a hospital and look after people who are sick.
Sometimes I work at night and sleep during the day.
Other times I have to start early in the morning. All the nurses at my hospital have to wear a uniform.
I can't drive, so I get the bus to work.

RADIO DJ

I work on a private radio station in Boston.
I have my own show from 2 pm to 5 pm.
I play some pop music and people call me to talk about the topics of the day.
I control the music and the callers with a special computer.
I love the radio – you can wear what you want, because nobody can see you!

2 Find out what Student B's job is by asking *Do you have to ......?* questions.

Student A: Do you have to wear special clothes?

Student B: No, I don't.

3 Now choose another job from the list below and let Student B try to find out what you are. Then, find out again what Student B's job is.

actor   engineer   farm worker
journalist   manager of a pop group
model   TV host   vet

Communication activity 4

Student A

1 Complete the quiz questions using the past participle of the verbs below. Then, find the answers.

create   declare   ~~discover~~   inhabit
lead   play

2 Ask Student B the questions in your quiz. Keep score.

QUIZ

1 What was discovered by Crick and Watson?
   a) DNA
   b) RNA
   c) NAD

2 What technique was Dolly the sheep ____ by?
   a) genetic reproduction
   b) cloning
   c) photocopying

3 What part of Australia is ____ by city-dwellers?
   a) the interior
   b) the coast
   c) the Outback

4 Who was the US Civil Rights Movement ____ by in the 1950s and 60s?
   a) President Johnson
   b) Martin Luther King
   c) Elvis Presley

5 What was ____ illegal in the USA by the Civil Rights Act in 1964?
   a) racial discrimination
   b) segregation in schools
   c) the Civil Rights Movement

6 What sport is ____ by the Chicago *Cubs*?
   a) baseball
   b) football
   c) basketball

Total score: ____

3 Answer Student B's quiz questions.

4 Now make up some quiz questions of your own to ask another student.

Communication activity 5

Student A

1 You and Student B are interviewing people about their opinions of various sports. Answer Student B's questions about what Amy told you.

Student B: What did Amy say about skateboarding?
Student A: She said she didn't like it.

SPORTS SURVEY

Name Amy

What do you think of:
Skateboarding? I don't like it.
Bungee jumping? It is very scary.
Scuba-diving? I do it each summer!
Hang-gliding? My brothers like it.
Kick-boxing? I love it!
Sky-diving? I don't have a good head for heights!

2 Now ask Student B what Martin said about these sports.

Name Martin

What do you think of:
Skateboarding?
Bungee jumping?
Scuba-diving?
Hang-gliding?
Kick-boxing?
Sky-diving?

3 What does Student B think of these sports? Ask him/her and report the answers back to the class.

Name

What do you think of:
Skateboarding?
Bungee jumping?
Scuba-diving?
Hang-gliding?
Kick-boxing?
Sky-diving?

Communication activity 6

Student A

1 What would they do? Ask and answer questions with Student B to complete the statements.

RICK
- If I was rich, I'd buy a ____
- If I lived in California, I'd go surfing every day.

EMILY
- If I could be any animal, I'd be a dolphin.
- If my boyfriend forgot my birthday, I'd ____

SUE
- If I lost my job, I'd have to ____
- If I didn't call home every day, my mom would get worried.

MARVIN
- If I crashed my dad's car, I'd ____
- If my girlfriend left me, I'd find another one.

Student A: What would Rick buy if he was rich?
Student B: He'd buy a ……

2 What would you do in those situations? Ask and answer with Student B.

Communication activity 1

Student B

Two students have applied for the same job in a music store.

ARE YOU A STUDENT?
Would you like a SUMMER JOB?
DAVE'S MUSIC, is looking for 1 STORE CLERK for the summer vacation.
5 days a week, including some Saturdays.
Driver's license would be an advantage.
Apply to Dave Gibson <dave@gibson.co.uk>

1 Read Sally's letter and answer Student A's questions.

> May 5 2002
> Dear Mr. Gibson,
> My name is Sally Ryan and I am eighteen years old. I saw your advert in the newspaper and I would really like to work in your store. I have worked part-time in a gas station since May last year. I am bored with it, and really need to change. I don't have a driver's license yet, but I am taking the test next month (I hope I pass!). My hobbies are basketball and listening to music (I like all types).
> Yours Sincerely,
> Sally Ryan

2 Ask Student A questions about Alan, and complete the form below.

What is his full name?
How old is he?
Has he worked before? Where? When?
Has he passed his driver's test? When?
What are his hobbies and interests?

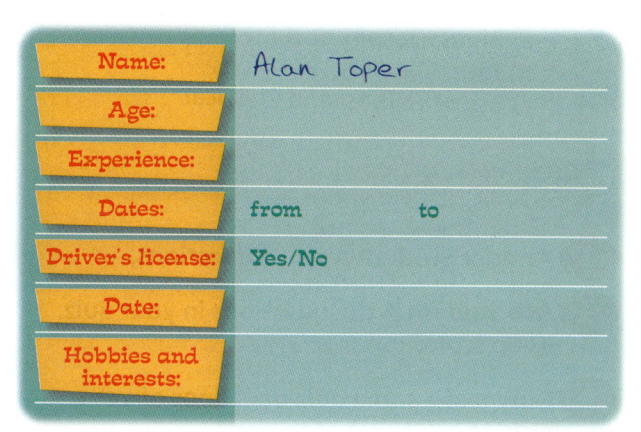

Name:	Alan Toper
Age:	
Experience:	
Dates:	from to
Driver's license:	Yes/No
Date:	
Hobbies and interests:	

3 Who do you think is the best candidate for the job? Why?

Communication activity 2

Student B

Anthony and Helen are doing a "treasure hunt" in New York. The first person to complete all the tasks on the list wins a prize.

1 Answer Student A's questions about what tasks Helen has completed.
   Student A: Has Helen taken a photo of Times Square yet?
   Student B: Yes, she has.

The New York City Treasure Hunt

Name: Helen Barker

Tasks:
- take a photo of Times Square ✓
- get the autograph of a New York bus driver ✓
- travel on the subway ☐
- cross the Hudson River ☐
- feed the ducks in Central Park ☐
- buy something with "I ♥ New York" on it ✓
- get a photo taken with a police officer ☐

2 Now ask Student A questions about Anthony.

The New York City Treasure Hunt

Name: Anthony Martin

Tasks:
- take a photo of Times Square ☐
- get the autograph of a New York bus driver ☐
- travel on the subway ☐
- cross the Hudson River ☐
- feed the ducks in Central Park ☐
- buy something with "I ♥ New York" on it ☐
- get a photo taken with a police officer ☐

3 Who do you think is going to win the treasure hunt?

Communication activity 3

Student B

1 Find out what Student A's job is by asking *Do you have to ……?* questions.

Student B: Do you have to wear special clothes?
Student A: Yes, I do.

WILDLIFE PHOTOGRAPHER

I travel around the world.
I take photos of animals in their natural environment.
I often have to get up early in the morning and drive to where the animals are.
I need to use a special camera. Sometimes I send pictures to my editor via my computer.

NURSE

I work in a hospital and look after people who are sick.
Sometimes I work at night, and sleep during the day.
Other times I have to start early in the morning. All the nurses at my hospital have to wear a uniform.
I can't drive, so I get the bus to work.

RADIO DJ

I work on a private radio station in Boston.
I have my own show from 2 pm to 5 pm.
I play some pop music, and people call me to talk about the topics of the day.
I control the music and the callers with a special computer.
I love the radio – you can wear what you want, because nobody can see you!

2 Now you choose a job, and answer Student A's questions.

3 Find out again what Student A's job is. Then, choose another job from the list below and let Student A try to find out what you are.

actor   engineer   farm worker
journalist   manager of a pop group
model   TV host   vet

Communication activity 4

Student B

1 Complete the quiz questions using the past participle of the verbs below. Then, find the answers.

call   commemorate   hear   inhabit
~~revolutionize~~   sign

QUIZ

1 What was revolutionized by Crick and Watson's discovery?
 a) life
 b) agriculture
 c) industry

2 What is ___ "the great leveler" by Australians?
 a) the Outback
 b) the sea
 c) the beach

3 Who was the Civil Rights Act ___ by in 1964?
 a) Martin Luther King
 b) President Johnson
 c) the police

4 What is Martin Luther King ___ by?
 a) the Nobel Prize
 b) A national holiday
 c) a gold medal

5 How many people is Chicago ___ by?
 a) under 2 million
 b) between 2 and 3 million
 c) over 3 million

6 What kind of music is ___ by audiences in Grant Park?
 a) Blues, Gospel, and Jazz
 b) Jazz, Classical, and Blues
 c) Gospel, Blues, and Classical

Total score: ___

2 Answer Student A's quiz questions.

3 Ask Student A the questions in your quiz. Keep score.

4 Now make some quiz questions of your own to ask another student.

Communication activity 5

Student B

1 You and Student A are interviewing people about their opinions of various sports. Ask Student A questions about what Amy thought of the sports (below).

Student B: What did Amy say about skateboarding?
Student A: She said she didn't like it.

SPORTS SURVEY

Name *Amy*

What do you think of:
Skateboarding?
Bungee jumping?
Scuba-diving?
Hang-gliding?
Kick-boxing?
Sky-diving?

2 Now read what Martin said, and answer Student A's questions.

Name *Martin*

What do you think of:
Skateboarding? *I love it.*
Bungee jumping? *It is very exciting.*
Scuba-diving? *My Dad likes it.*
Hang-gliding? *My cousins often do it.*
Kick-boxing? *I don't like it at all.*
Sky-diving? *I think its great.*

3 What does Student A think of these sports? Ask him/her and report the answers back to the class.

Name

What do you think of:
Skateboarding?
Bungee jumping?
Scuba-diving?
Hang-gliding?
Kick-boxing?
Sky-diving?

Communication activity 6

Student B

1 What would they do? Ask and answer questions with Student A to complete the statements.

RICK: If I was rich, I'd buy a big house in the United States.
If I lived in California, I'd ___.

EMILY: If I could be any animal, I'd be a ___.
If my boyfriend forgot my birthday, I'd leave him.

SUE: If I lost my job, I'd have to move back with my parents.
If I didn't call home every day, my mom would ___.

MARVIN: If I crashed my dad's car, I'd leave the country.
If my girlfriend left me, I'd ___.

Student B: What would Rick do if he lived in California?
Student A: He'd......

2 What would you do in those situations? Ask and answer with Student A.

NUMBER ONE

Carla Johnson is 16. She's lived in Boston with her dad and brother Darren since she was ten. The Johnsons moved there from Cape Cod after Carla's mother died. Peter and Darren Johnson are both fishermen ...

Darren! If you don't hurry up, we'll be late!

OK, I'm coming.

Bye!

Carla graduated two weeks ago. In September she's going to start work in a local grocery store, but she doesn't really want a grocery store job. She wants to be a pop singer. Later that morning ...

"I'm the one who loves you. Every day it makes me proud, Just to stand beside you. You're my sky without a cloud."

That evening

What do you think, Dad? I'm sending my tape and this letter to Supersounds – a big record company in New York.

"I'm the one who loves you ..."

Dear Sir or Madam, My name's CJ. I hope you like the tape that I'm sending you. I've been singing for five years now and it's my dream to be a pop star.

That's great, Carla. This tape's amazing, too. Well done!

Two weeks later.

Dad! Darren!

Dear Carla, I really enjoyed your tape. Can you come to New York on July 12 at 2 pm? Every summer we see six exciting young singers and give one of them a special "Star of Tomorrow" contract. We'd like you to be one of our six singers this year. Best wishes, Paula Monroe Managing Director, Supersounds

Carla, this is fantastic! I haven't been so happy since ...

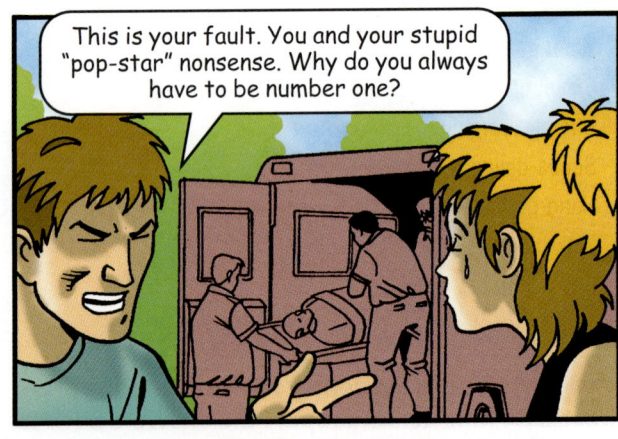

But then ...

Aarrghh

Dad!

Call an ambulance! Use your cell phone! QUICKLY!

This is your fault. You and your stupid "pop-star" nonsense. Why do you always have to be number one?

Next day ...

I need a heart operation. The doctors are going to do it next Wednesday.

That's July 12. OK – I'll call Supersounds and say "I'm sorry but I can't come."

No. If you do that, you'll lose your big chance. Go to New York, Carla. I'll be fine.

On July 12 Carla arrives at the offices of Supersounds.

SUPERSOUNDS
Los Angeles – New York – London – Paris

Half an hour later she gets a text message.

Carla Johnson?

Good luck! Dad.

So, CJ
Carla sings for Paula Monroe. After that she has to wait for two hours. Paula Monroe talks to the five other singers one by one, then finally ...
"Brr, Brr ..."
Oh, please excuse me, Ms Monroe. It's my brother. This is a very important call.
Carla? I've just spoken to the doctors. Everything went well and Dad's OK.
Oh, Darren, that's great news.
Sorry
No problem. Anyway, I have great news, too. Supersounds want YOU to be our Star of Tomorrow!
Honestly!?
Yes, and we have a perfect song for you. It's called "Number One". You can record it next week, and we'll release it in the fall. Until then you can stay at our Supersounds apartment.
Two months later, Carla's getting ready for her first TV show, Poptastic! She's very nervous. Then ...
Dad! Darren! You've arrived!
Hello, sweetheart.
Wow! You look great Carla.
How are you?
Much better. There's only one problem now. The doctors won't let me work on the boat any more, so I have no job.
Maybe I can help. Would you like to be my manager? After all, you've helped me all my life. Now, finally, I can help you!
But ... I don't know anything about the music business!
CJ - Two minutes.
You can always learn.
You're right. OK, I'll do it.
You're my number one - The biggest hit there's ever been
You're my number one - The brightest star there's ever been,
Oh, yeah.

Comprehension

Do these exercises about *Number One*.

1 Match the pictures (a–h) with the people and places (1–8).
1. Carla Johnson — c
2. Darren Johnson ___
3. Peter Johnson ___
4. Paula Monroe ___
5. Carla's bedroom ___
6. Dad and Darren's fishing boat ___
7. The Johnson's kitchen ___
8. The offices at *Supersounds* ___

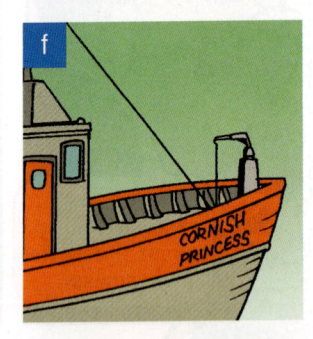

2 Who says (or writes) these sentences, and to whom?

If you don't hurry up, we'll be late.
Dad to Darren

1. Why do you always have to be number one?
2. I hope you like the tape that I'm sending you.
3. Can you come to New York on July 12 at 2 pm?
4. *Supersounds* want YOU to be our "Star of Tomorrow".
5. The doctors won't let me work on the boat any more, so I have no job.
6. Would you like to be my manager?

3 Put the events in the story (a–f) in the correct order (1–6).

Order	1	2	3	4	5	6
Event	f	__	__	__	__	__

a) *Supersounds* invite Carla to take part in their "Star of Tomorrow" contest.
b) Carla appears on *Poptastic*!
c) Mr. Johnson collapses.
d) Carla graduates.
e) Mr. Johnson has an operation.
f) The Johnsons move from Cape Cod to Boston.

4 Answer these questions about the story.

How long has Carla lived in Boston?
For six years.

1. What kind of work does her brother do?
2. What are a) *Megahits* b) *Supersounds* c) *Poptastic*?
3. Who is Paula Monroe?
4. Two things happen on July 12 – What are they?
5. Why do you think the story is called *Number One*?

5 You're a journalist for *Megahits* magazine. Write a short article about CJ. Describe her new single – *Number One* – and her appearance on *Poptastic*.

6 It's now six months later. What do you think has happened since CJ appeared on *Poptastic* to:
1. Carla herself?
2. Her father?
3. Darren?

MOUNTAIN MYSTERY!

Zack Tyler lives in Denver, Colorado. He loves cars, sports and climbing. One weekend in October, his parents are invited to a wedding in San Francisco.

"The cab's here, Joan. Hurry up or we'll miss our flight."

"Here are the car keys, Zack. have fun, but be careful and don't do anything stupid, OK?"

The cab leaves, then Zack calls his best friend, Tom Holden.

"Tom, Hi. Listen, do you want to go climbing in the Rockies tomorrow?"

"Sure, but I'll have to ask my parents first."

Two minutes later ...

"They say that I can go."

"Great! I'll pick you up tomorrow morning at nine."

"This book is amazing. It says that spirits and strange creatures are often seen by mountain climbers."

"Yeah, right! Big Foot, the Yeti? Come on, Tom – no one believes in that!"

Later ...

"If I was rich, I'd never work. I'd do this each day instead."

"Have you seen those black clouds, Zack? The weather's changing."

Five minutes later, something terrible happens.

Tom!

WAAAHHH!!!!

Luckily, Tom lands on some deep snow.

"It's my leg. I think it's broken."

"Hello? HELLO??"

"My phone's not working. The battery must be dead."

The boys hide in a cave for two days. It snows constantly. Then ...

"Where are you going?"

"To get help. You need a doctor, Tom. We've waited long enough."

"But look at the weather. You can't be serious."

Meanwhile, five miles away ...

"Tom Holden's parents said that the boys left Denver on Saturday morning. That was 48 hours ago. Earlier today, Police Chief Don Drake told reporters "Everything possible is being done, but conditions here are extremely bad." This is Connie Chan for CBC News."

Three hours later Tom sees something strange in the cave. It's a woman carrying some wood.

I must be dreaming!

She carefully puts down the wood. Then...

How did you...? Who ARE you?

But at that moment...

Two hours later...

Chaka chaka

It's no good Tom. I couldn't find anyone, the snow's too... Wait! What's that noise?

Help! HELP!

Look! There's someone down there.

The paramedic is lowered to the ground. He looks at Tom's leg.

Don't worry, Tom. We'll be back home soon and you'll be fine.

It's badly broken in three places.

Ten minutes later in the helicopter.

Tell me something, Tom. When I got back there was a fire in the cave. How did you make it?

I didn't. It was made by a woman.

A woman? What woman?

Tom explains...

But that doesn't make sense. People don't just disappear!

And you guys were near the summit. There are no trees that high. Where did she find the wood?

Your leg isn't broken any more!

Ahhh!!

That's impossible!

It may not be possible... but it's true.

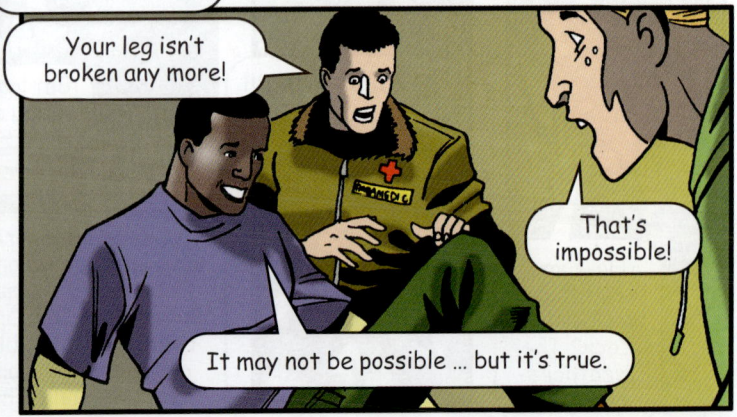

Comprehension

Do these exercises about *Mountain Mystery*.

1 Match the pictures (a–h) with the people (1–8).
1 Zack Tyler _g_
2 Tom Holden ___
3 Connie Chan ___
4 The mystery woman ___
5 The helicopter pilot ___
6 Joan Tyler ___
7 The paramedic ___
8 Zack's father ___

2 Who says these sentences and to whom?

Have fun, but be careful and don't do anything stupid, OK?
Joan Tyler to Zack

1 They say that I can go!
2 If I was rich, I'd never work.
3 Everything possible is being done, but conditions here are extremely bad.
4 There's someone down there.
5 We'll be back home soon and you'll be fine.
6 It may not be possible … but it's true.

3 Put these events in the story (a–f) in the correct order (1–6).

Order	1	2	3	4	5	6
Event	c	__	__	__	__	__

a) Tom sees a mysterious woman.
b) Zack asks Tom to go climbing.
c) Zack's parents go away for the weekend.
d) Zack and Tom are seen by the helicopter pilot.
e) Tom breaks his leg.
f) The paramedic says that Tom's leg isn't broken any more.

4 Answer these questions about the story.

Why did Zack's parents go away for the weekend?
They were going to a wedding in San Francisco.

1 What is *Mountain Mysteries*?
2 After Tom's fall, Zack is unable to call for help. Why?
3 Two days later, Zack leaves Tom on his own. Why?
4 Who is Connie Chan?
5 What does Police Chief Don Drake tell reporters?

5 You're a newspaper journalist. Zack and Tom have just returned from the Rockies and told their story at a press conference. Now it's your turn. Write a short article for your paper about the boys' amazing adventure.

6 What do you think? Discuss these questions with your friends.

1 Who (or what) was the woman in the cave?
2 Will the people who hear about Tom's story in the media believe it? Why?/Why not?

Grammar help

Units 1 and 2

Simple past

Regular verbs (affirmative)

a Most verbs: subject + base form of verb + **-ed**
  Simon **opened** the door.
  We **opened** the letters.

b Verbs ending with **e**: subject + base form of verb + **-d**
  She **closed** the window.

c Some verbs ending with one vowel and one consonant: subject + base form, double the consonant + **-ed**
  They **stopped** reading.

d Verbs ending with **y:** subject + base form ~~y~~ + **-ied**
  He **studied** French in college.

Irregular verbs (affirmative)
Subject + irregular simple past

I **forgot** your address.
They **won** the contest.
Louise **wrote** a poem.

There are no rules about how to make simple past forms of irregular verbs, so you will have to learn them.

Regular and irregular verbs (negative)
Subject + **did not/didn't** + base form of verb
He **didn't enjoy** the concert.

Regular and irregular verbs (question forms and short answers)

Question forms
Did + subject + base form of verb

Short answers
Yes, + subject + **did**.
No, + subject + **didn't**.

Did you **watch** TV last night? **Yes**, I **did**.
Did she **answer** the question? **No**, she **didn't**.

We usually use contracted forms for negative short answers.

Present perfect

Affirmative
subject + **has/have** + past participle
She **has eaten** lunch.

Negative
subject + **has/have not (hasn't/haven't)** + past participle
I **haven't done** my homework.
Jane **hasn't tidied** her room.

*We can use **never** in negative sentences with the present perfect. **Never** means "not in my/your/his/her/their life" and we put it before the past participle.*

I**'ve never been** to Africa.
He**'s never broken** an arm or leg.

Question forms
Has/Have + subject + past participle

Short answers
Yes, + subject + **has/have**.
No, + subject + **hasn't/haven't**.

Have you **seen** this movie? **Yes**, I **have**.
Has she **lost** her keys again? **No**, she **hasn't**.

We always use full forms for affirmative short answers. We usually use contracted forms for negative short answers.
*We can use **ever** in questions with the present perfect. **Ever** means "in my/your/his/her/their life", and we put it before the past participle.*

Have you **ever swum** with a dolphin?
Has Pete **ever run** a marathon?

Simple past and present perfect

We use the **simple past** and the **present perfect** to talk about the past. But:
1. We use the **simple past** to describe actions completed at a specific time in the past.

completed action	specific time
Sally **drank** some milk	before bed.
I **saw** a good movie on TV	yesterday.
He **didn't go** to the movies	last week.

2. We use the **present perfect**:
   a. to talk about experiences and the number of times we have experienced them.

I'**ve been** to Australia twice in my life.

   b. to connect the past with the present.

event in the past	effect in the present
I'**ve** already **eaten**.	(... so I'm not hungry now.)
He'**s finished** his homework.	(... so he can go out now.)

Relative pronouns *who*, *which/that*, and *whose*

We can use **relative pronouns** to join two sentences together.

A pilot is a person.	→	A pilot is a person
He flies a plane.		**who** flies a plane.
A cow is an animal.	→	A cow is an animal
It eats grass.		**that** eats grass.

We use the relative pronoun **who** for people.

A pianist is a person.	→	A pianist is a person
He plays the piano.		**who** plays the piano.
A florist is a person.	→	A florist is a person
She sells flowers.		**who** sells flowers.

We use the relative pronouns **which** or **that** for animals and things.

A mouse is an animal.	→	A mouse is an animal
It likes cheese.		**which** likes cheese.
A lawnmower is a machine.	→	A lawnmower is a machine
It cuts grass.		**that** cuts grass.

We use the relative pronoun **whose** to talk about possession.

My father is a writer.	→	My father is a writer
His books are popular		**whose** books are popular
in Japan.		in Japan.

Units 3 and 4

Present perfect with *for* and *since*

We can use **for** and **since** with the present perfect. We use **for** with a period of time.

She has lived here **for three years**.

We use **since** with a point in time.

She has lived here **since 2004**.

Present perfect with *just, already, yet*

We can use **just, already**, and **yet** with the present perfect. We usually use **just** and **already** in affirmative sentences. They go between **have/has** and the past participle. **Just** means "very recently" and **already** means "earlier than expected"

I've **just** bought a new computer.
Peter and Sam have **just** gotten some new plates but they've **already** broken two of them.

We usually use **yet** in negative sentences and questions. It goes at the end of the sentence. In negative sentences, we use **yet** to say that something which is expected is in the future, not the present or the past. In questions, we use **yet** to ask if something which is expected has happened.

Justin Timberlake has recorded a new CD but I haven't heard it **yet**.
Have you seen the new Spielberg movie **yet**?

Adverbs of manner

To make most adverbs, we start with the adjective. There are five groups of adverbs:

	adjective		adverb
Group 1: add **-ly** to the adjective	bad quick polite	→ → →	bad**ly** quick**ly** polite**ly**
Group 2: remove **-y** from the adjective and add **-ily**	angry easy noisy	→ → →	angr**ily** eas**ily** nois**ily**
Group 3: add **-ally** to the adjective	tragic fantastic	→ →	tragic**ally** fantastic**ally**
Group 4: the adverb is the same as the adjective	early fast hard late	→ → → →	**early** **fast** **hard** **late**
Group 5: irregular	good	→	**well**

We usually use adverbs with verbs. We use **adverbs of manner** to describe how somebody does something.

He closed the door **quietly**.
The train arrived **late**.
Jane is good at driving – she drives **well**.

Units 5 and 6

Conditionals

Conditionals have two parts: an **If** clause and a main clause.
When the **If** clause comes first, we use a comma between the two clauses.

If clause	main clause
If you press this button,	the window opens.

When the main clause comes first, we don't use a comma.

main clause	*If* clause
The window opens	if you press this button.

Zero conditional

In zero conditionals, we use the **simple present** for the **If** clause and for the main clause.
We use **zero conditionals** to express facts that are always true.

If you **drop** an egg, it **breaks**.
If you **heat** ice, it **melts**.

First conditional

In first conditionals, we use the **simple present** for the **If** clause, and the **future with will** for the main clause.
We use **first conditionals** to express predictions about the future, to describe things that will possibly happen.

If you **break** that, I **will be** angry!

have to (affirmative)

| I/we/you/they | have to | clean the kitchen this |
| he/she/it | has to | afternoon. |

I **have to** work this weekend.
Peter **has to** wash the car tomorrow.

We usually use full forms for affirmative sentences with **have to**.
We use **have to** in the affirmative to express obligation.

I **have to** go to work at 9 o'clock. (… because my employer says so)

have to (negative)

I/we/you/they	do not have to / don't have to	make dinner tonight.
he/she/it	does not have to / doesn't have to	

> We use **have to** in the negative to express a lack of obligation.

I **don't have to** be at the party until 9 o'clock.
(… because the party doesn't start until 9 o'clock)

have to (question forms)

Do	I/we/you/they	have to	go shopping tomorrow?
Does	he/she/it		

have to (short answers)

Affirmative

Yes,	I/we/you/they	do.
	he/she/it	does.

Negative

No,	I/we/you/they	don't.
	he/she/it	doesn't.

Do you **have to** take the dog for a walk?
Yes, I do.
Does he **have to** open the door for her?
No, he doesn't.

> We usually use contracted forms for negative short answers.

need

I/we/you/they	need	to buy a new coat.
he/she/it	needs	

> We use **need** to express necessity.

I **need to** go to the doctor's. (… because I'm sick)
You **need to** sign this form. (= It is necessary to sign this form.)

Units 7 and 8

Passive

To make an active sentence into a passive sentence:
1 we make the **object** of the active sentence into the **subject** of the passive sentence.
2 we change the **main verb** in the active sentence into the correct tense of **be + the past participle** of the main verb. For example, if the main verb in the active sentence is in the simple present, we use **be** in the simple present in the passive sentence.

Active			
subject	simple present of the main verb	object	
People	make	these cars	in Japan.
Passive			
subject	simple present of *be*	past participle of the main verb	
These cars	are	made	in Japan.

And if the main verb in the active sentence is in the simple past, we use **be** in the simple past in the passive sentence.

Active			
subject	simple past of the main verb	object	
She	called	me	at 10 o'clock.
Passive			
subject	simple past of *be*	past participle of the main verb	
I	was	called	at 10 o'clock.

When we want to say what people or things do, we use active sentences. However, when we want to say what happens to people or things, we usually use passive sentences.
We can use the passive with **by** + agent when it's important to know who does the action.

Active
Picasso **painted** this picture.

Passive
This picture **was painted by** Picasso.

Logical deductions: *must be, can't be*

We use **must be** in affirmative sentences to say that we are sure that something is true.

She's crying – she **must be** upset.
They've won all their games – they **must be** very good players.

We use **can't be** in negative sentences to say that we are sure something is not true.

She's crying – she **can't be** happy.
They've lost all their games – they **can't be** very good players.

Units 9 and 10

Reported speech: with reporting verbs in the *present*

To make direct speech into reported speech:
1 we sometimes change the tenses of the verbs:
*If the verbs in direct speech are in the **present** and the reporting verb (**say/tell**) is in the **present**, then the verbs in reported speech are also in the **present**.*

Direct speech	Reported speech
David, now: I'm hungry. →	David **says** (that) he's hungry.

Reported speech: with reporting verbs in the *past*

*If the verbs in direct speech are in the **present** but the reporting verb (**said/told**) is in the **past**, then the verbs in reported speech change to the **past**.*

Direct speech	Reported speech
David, in the past: I'm hungry. →	David **said** (that) he **was** hungry.

2 we sometimes change the pronouns and possessive adjectives:

Direct speech	Reported speech
Mark: **I** don't like chocolate. →	Mark says **he** doesn't like chocolate.
Jane: He can see **me**. →	Jane says he can see **her**.
Sarah and Kim: Peter helped **us**. →	Sarah and Kim say that Peter helped **them**.
Jeff and Sam: That's **our** car. →	Jeff and Sam said that was **their** car.
Jane: **My** friend likes pizza. →	Jane said that **her** friend liked pizza.
Peter, to me: I like **your** jacket. →	Peter said that **he** liked **my** jacket.
Peter, to Jane: I like **your** jacket. →	Peter told Jane that **he** liked **her** jacket.

Indefinite pronouns

someone	something
anyone	anything
no one	nothing

*We use **indefinite pronouns** when we can't or don't want to talk about a particular person or thing.*

Someone has drunk my coffee! (… I don't know who)
Can **anyone** help me? (… it doesn't matter who)
There's **something** wrong with my car. (… I don't know what)

*We usually use **someone** and **something** in affirmative sentences.*

Someone has taken my coat.
He took **something** out of the box.

*We usually use **anyone** and **anything** in questions and negative sentences.*

Has **anyone** seen my cat?
I can't see **anything**.

Units 11 and 12

Second conditional

> In second conditionals, we use the **simple past** for the **If** clause and **would + infinitive** for the main clause.

If I **won** a lot of money, I **would buy** a house in Barbados.
If you **lost** your job, what **would** you **do**?
I **would be** very unhappy if you **left**.
If he **got** a new job, he **wouldn't** move house.

> We use **second conditionals** to express things that probably won't happen.

first conditional
If you break that, I will be angry! (= I think you probably will break it.)
second conditional
If you broke that, I would be angry! (= I don't think you will break it.)

Possessive pronouns

Possessive adjective		Possessive pronoun
my	→	mine
your	→	yours
his	→	his
her	→	hers
its	→	its
our	→	ours
your	→	yours
their	→	theirs

> We can use **possessive pronouns** when we don't want to repeat a possessive adjective + noun.

Whose is this hat? It's **mine**. (= It's my hat.)
I didn't bring a pen, so Sarah lent me **hers**. (= … her pen)
He has his books and we have **ours**. (= … our books)

Whose …?

> We use **whose …?** to ask about possession, to ask who owns something.

Whose is this coat? It's Peter's. (= Who owns this coat?)
Whose are these boots? They're mine. (= Who owns these boots?)

Bonus units

Past perfect (affirmative)

| I/you/he/she/it/we/you/they | had | closed
done
finished |

*We make the past perfect with **had** + the **past participle** of the main verb.*

I **had seen** the movie before.
They **had lost** their shoes.

Past perfect (negative)

| I/you/he/she/it/we/you/they | had not
hadn't | closed
done
finished |

I **hadn't finished** my lunch!
We **hadn't opened** our bags yet.

Past perfect (question forms)

| Had | I/you/he/she/it/we/you/they | closed …?
done …?
finished …? |

Past perfect (short answers)

| Yes, | I/you/he/she/it/we/you/they | had. |
| No, | I/you/he/she/it/we/you/they | hadn't. |

Had you **been** to the swimming pool before?
Yes, I **had**.
Had they **seen** the Taj Mahal?
No, they **hadn't**.

We always use full forms for affirmative short answers. We usually use contracted forms for negative short answers.
*We use the **past perfect** to describe a past action that happened before another event in the past.*

After I **had seen** the game, I went home.
(= I saw the game first, then I went home.)
He left the house when he **had done** the dishes.
(= He did the dishes, then he left the house.)

The reporting verbs *say* and *tell*

*We can use the verbs **say** and **tell** to introduce reported speech.*

Direct speech		Reported speech
Mike: I like fast cars.	→	Mike **said** (that) he liked fast cars.
Mike, to Peter: I like fast cars.	→	Mike **told** Peter (that) he liked fast cars.

*We use **say** when there is no personal object.* | *We use **tell** when there is a personal object.*

He **said** he had spaghetti for lunch.	He **told me** he had spaghetti for lunch.
She **said** she was unhappy.	She **told her friend** that she was unhappy.
They **said** that I was wrong.	They **told Susan** that I was wrong.

Third conditional

*In third conditionals, we use **had** + the past participle in the **If** clause and **would have** + the past participle in the main clause.*
*We use the **third conditional** when we imagine a situation in the past which did not happen.*

He **would have come** to the party if you'**d invited** him. (… but you didn't invite him, so he didn't come)
If you'**d told** me the club was closed, I **wouldn't have gone** there. (… but you didn't tell me, so I went)

Too and *enough*

*We can use **too** and **not … enough** with adjectives. Note that we put **too** before the adjective and **enough** after the adjective.*

| This shirt is **too small**. | = | This shirt is**n't big enough**. |
| My pants are **too short**. | = | My pants are**n't long enough**. |

Word list

- **Let's remember**
  - **Kinds of transportation**
    - bike /baik/
    - boat /bout/
    - bus /bəs/
    - (on) foot /fʊt/
    - helicopter /ˈheliˌkaptər/
    - motorcycle /ˈmoutərˌsaikəl/
    - plane /plein/
    - ship /ʃɪp/
    - train /trein/
    - truck /trək/
  - **Towns and Buildings**
    - bank /bæŋk/
    - bookstore /ˈbʊkstər/
    - bus station /ˈbəs steiʃən/
    - church /tʃərtʃ/
    - grocery store /ˈgrous(ə)ri stər/
    - movie theatre /ˈmuvi ˈθiətər, θiˈeitər/
    - museum /myuˈziəm/
    - park /park/
    - post office /ˈpoust ˌɔfɪs/
  - **In the restaurant**
    - appetizer /ˈæpəˌtaizər/
    - fork /fɔrk/
    - glass /glæs/
    - juice /dʒus/
    - knife /naif/
    - main course /mein ˈkɔrs/
    - napkin /ˈnæpkɪn/
    - pepper /ˈpepər/
    - salt /sɔlt/
    - soup /sup/
    - spoon /spun/
    - tablecloth /ˈteibəlklɔθ/
    - waiter /ˈweitər/
  - **Describing people: personality**
    - cheap /tʃip/
    - cheerful /ˈtʃɪrfəl/
    - confident /ˈkanfədənt/
    - generous /ˈdʒen(ə)rəs/
    - hard-working /hard ˈwərkɪŋ/
    - impatient /ɪmˈpeiʃənt/
    - lazy /ˈleizi/
    - mean /min/
    - modest /ˈmadɪst/
    - patient /ˈpeiʃənt/
    - polite /pəˈlait/
    - rude /rud/
    - sad /sæd/
    - shy /ʃai/
    - vain /vein/
  - **Personal computers**
    - DVD /di vi ˈdi/
    - floppy disk /ˈflapi ˈdɪsk/
    - keyboard /ˈkibɔrd/
    - modem /ˈmoudem/
    - monitor /ˈmanətər/
    - mouse /maus/
    - mouse pad /ˈmaus pæd/
    - speakers /ˈspikərz/

- **Unit 1**
  - **Expressions**
    - It's on me! /ɪts an ˈmi/
    - Stop quarrelling! /stap ˈkwɔrəlɪŋ/
    - Thanks for the offer. /θæŋks fər ðə ˈɔfər/
    - You're right! /yʊr ˈrait/

- **Unit 2**
  - **Culture**
    - flock /flak/
    - gourmet /ˈgʊrˌmei/
    - inspire /ɪnˈspaiər/
    - nut /nət/
    - population /ˌpapyəˈleiʃən/
    - settle /ˈsetəl/
  - **British English and American English**
    - autumn/fall /ˈɔtəm, fɔl/
    - biscuits/cookies /ˈbɪskɪts, ˈkʊkiz/
    - cinema/movie theater /ˈsɪnəmə, ˈmuvi ˈθiətər, θiˈeitər/
    - crisps/chips /krɪsps, tʃɪpz/
    - film/movie /fɪlm, ˈmuvi/
    - flat/apartment /flæt, əˈpartmənt/
    - ground floor/first floor /graund flɔr, ˈfərst flɔr/
    - holiday/vacation /ˈholəˌdei, veiˈkeiʃən/
    - lift/elevator /lɪft, ˈeləˌveitər/
    - mobile phone/cell phone /ˈmoubəl, -ˌbiəl, -ˌbaiəl ˈfoun, sel foun/
    - motorway/highway /ˈmoutərwei, ˈhaiwei/
    - pavement/sidewalk /ˈpeivmənt, ˈsaidwɔk/
    - petrol/gas /ˈpetrəl, gæs/
    - queue/line /kyu, lain/
    - shop/store /ʃap, stɔr/
    - sweets/candy /switz, ˈkændi/
    - taxi/cab /ˈtæksi, kæb/
    - underground/subway /ˈəndərˌgraund, ˈsəbˌwei/

- **Unit 3**
  - **Expressions**
    - But his dad won't let him. /bət hɪz dæd wount ˈlet hɪm/
    - She's crazy about him. /ʃiz ˈkreizi əˈbaut hɪm/
    - What's it like? /(h)watz, (h)wətz ɪt ˈlaik/
    - You look great! /yu lʊk ˈgreit/

- **Unit 4**
  - **Culture**
    - achievement /əˈtʃivmənt/
    - admit /ədˈmɪt/
    - commemorate /kəˈmeməˌreit/
    - considerable /kənˈsɪdərəbəl/
    - declare /dɪˈklær/
    - mourn /mɔrn/
    - resistance /rɪˈzɪstəns/
    - spread /spred/
  - **Feelings and emotions**
  - **Nouns**
    - anger /ˈæŋgər/
    - confidence /ˈkanfədəns/
    - envy /ˈenvi/
    - fear /fɪr/
    - happiness /ˈhæpinɪs/
    - jealousy /ˈdʒeləsi/
    - pride /praid/
    - sadness /ˈsædnɪs/
  - **Adjectives**
    - afraid /əˈfreid/
    - angry /ˈæŋgri/
    - confident /ˈkanfədənt/
    - envious /ˈenviəs/
    - happy /ˈhæpi/
    - jealous /ˈdʒeləs/
    - proud /praud/
    - sad /sæd/

Unit 5

- **Expressions**
  Guys /gaiz/
  in any case /ɪn 'eni keis/
  one day /wən dei/
  That's incredible /ðætz ɪn'kredəbəl/

Unit 6

- **Culture**
  carry on /ˌkæri 'an/
  city-dweller /'sɪti dwelər/
  go snorkelling /gou 'snɔrkəlɪŋ/
  leveller /'levələr/
  outback /'autˌbæk/
  revolve /rɪ'valv/
  variety /və'raɪəti/
  vast /væst/

- **Verbs**
  agree/disagree /ə'gri, dɪsə'gri/
  appear/disappear /ə'pɪr, dɪsə'pɪr/

- **Adjectives**
  complete/incomplete /kəm'plit, ˌɪnkəm'plit/
  correct/incorrect /kə'rekt, ˌɪnkə'rekt/
  dependent/independent /di'pendənt, ˌɪndɪ'pendənt/
  finite/infinite /'faɪˌnaɪt, 'ɪnfənɪt/
  fortunate/unfortunate /'fɔrtʃənət, ˌən'fɔrtʃənət/
  honest/dishonest /'anɪst, dɪs'anɪst/
  kind/unkind /kaɪnd, ˌən'kaɪnd/
  legal/illegal /'ligəl, ɪ'ligəl/
  liberal/illiberal /'lɪb(ə)rəl, ɪ'lɪbrəl/
  literate/illiterate /'lɪtərɪt, ɪ'lɪtərɪt/
  logical/illogical /'ladʒɪkəl, ɪ'ladʒɪkəl/
  mobile/immobile /'moubəl, -ˌbɪəl, -ˌbaɪəl, ɪ'moubəl, -ˌbɪəl, -ˌbaɪəl/
  moral/immoral /'mɔrəl, ɪ'mɔrəl/
  obedient/disobedient /ou'bɪdiənt, ˌdɪsə'bidiənt/
  patient/impatient /'peɪʃənt, ɪm'peɪʃənt/
  pleasant/unpleasant /'plezənt, ˌən'plezənt/
  possible/impossible /'pasəbəl, ɪm'pasəbəl/
  regular/irregular /'regyələr, ɪ'regyələr/
  relevant/irrelevant /'reləvənt, ɪ'reləvənt/
  replaceable/irreplaceable /rɪ'pleɪsəbəl, ɪrɪ'pleɪsəbəl/
  responsible/irresponsible /rɪ'spansəbəl, ɪrɪ'spansəbəl/
  tidy/untidy /'taɪdi, ˌən'taɪdi/
  visible/invisible /'vɪzəbəl, 'ɪn'vɪzəbəl/

Unit 7

- **Expressions**
  Good for him! /'gʊd fər hɪm/
  If you're lucky. /ɪf yɔr 'ləki/
  Oh, I hope so. /ou aɪ 'houp sou/
  You can't be serious. /yu kænt bi 'sɪriəs/

Unit 8

- **Culture**
  clone /kloun/
  crops /kraps/
  incredibly /ɪn'kredəbli/
  raise /reɪz/
  recipe /'resəpi/
  revolutionize /ˌrevə'luʃəˌnaɪz/
  species /'spiˌʃiz/

- **Suffixes**

- **Nouns**
  actress /'æktrɪs/
  agreement /ə'grimənt/
  artist /'artɪst/
  boxer /'baksər/
  capitalism /'kæpətəˌlɪzəm/
  capitalist /'kæpətəˌlɪst/
  collection /kə'lekʃən/
  communism /'kamyəˌnɪzəm/
  communist /'kamyəˌnɪzt/
  darkness /'darknɪs/
  disappointment /ˌdɪsə'pɔɪntmənt/
  embarrassment /ɪm'bærəsmənt/
  employee /ˌem'plɔɪ(y)i/
  entertainment /ˌentər'teɪnmənt/
  farmer /'farmər/
  information /ˌɪnfər'meɪʃən/
  kindness /'kaɪndnɪs/
  lioness /'laɪənɪs/
  photographer /fə'tagrəfər/
  sexism /'sekˌsɪzəm/
  smoothness /'smuðnɪs/
  socialism /'souʃəˌlɪzəm/
  socialist /'souʃəˌlɪst/
  waitress /'weɪtrɪs/

- **Adjectives**
  Egyptian /i'dʒɪpʃən/
  faithful /'feɪθfəl/
  helpful /'helpfəl/
  helpless /'helplɪs/
  hopeful /'houpfəl/
  hopeless /'houplɪs/
  Japanese /dʒæpə'niz/
  penniless /'penɪlɪs, 'penəlɪs/
  Polish /'poulɪʃ/
  priestess /pris'tes/
  useful /'yusfəl/
  useless /'yuslɪs/

Unit 9

- **Expressions**
  Great news! /greɪt 'nuz/
  I'll be back home ... /aɪəl bi bæk 'houm/
  Oh! Yuck! /ou 'yək/
  What about you? /(h)wat, (h)wət ə'baʊt 'yu/

Unit 10

- **Culture**
  appoint /ə'pɔɪnt/
  coach /koutʃ/
  compete /kəm'pit/
  onwards /'anwərds/
  solid /'salɪd/
  tournament /'tɜrnəmənt/

- **Sports**
  abseiling /'æbseɪəlɪŋ/
  bungee jumping /'bəndʒi dʒəmpɪŋ/
  hang-gliding /'hæŋ glaɪdɪŋ/
  jet-skiing /'dʒet skiɪŋ/
  kick-boxing /kɪk baksɪŋ/
  scuba-diving /'skubə daɪvɪŋ/
  skateboarding /'skeɪt bɔrdɪŋ/
  sky-diving /skaɪ daɪvɪŋ/
  snowboarding /'snou bɔrdɪŋ/

Unit 11

- **Expressions**
  Cheers! Here's to you! /tʃɪrz 'hɪrz tə yu/
  Don't be such a coward! /dount bi setʃ ə 'kouərd/
  I feel kind of sad. /aɪ 'fɪəl kaɪnd əv sæd/
  Well done! /wel 'dən/

Unit 12

- **Culture**
  abbreviation /əˌbriviˈeiʃən/
  extreme /ikˈstrim/
  include /inˈklud/
  native /ˈneitiv/
  punctuation /ˌpəŋktʃuˈeiʃən/
  screen /skrin/

- **Word families**

- **Nouns**
  actor /ˈæktər/
  arrival /əˈraivəl/
  discussion /diˈskəʃən/
  fortune /ˈfɔrtʃən/
  happiness /ˈhæpinis/
  help /help/
  honesty /ˈanisti/
  hope /houp/
  origin /ˈɔrədʒin/
  politeness /pəˈlaitnis/
  possibility /ˌpasəˈbiləti/
  use /yus/

- **Verbs**
  act /ˈækt/
  argue /ˈarˌgyu/
  arrive /əˈraiv/
  discuss /diˈskəs/
  help /help/
  hope /houp/
  originate /əˈridʒəˌneit/
  use /yuz/

- **Adjectives**
  confident /ˈkanfədənt/
  fortunate /ˈfɔrtʃənət/
  happy /ˈhæpi/
  helpful /helpfəl/
  helpless /helplis/
  honest /ˈanist/
  hopeful /houpfəl/
  hopeless /houplis/
  original /əˈridʒənəl/
  polite /pəˈlait/
  possible /ˈpasəbəl/
  useful /yusfəl/
  useless /yuslis/

- **Adverbs**
  confidently /ˈkanfədəntli/
  fortunately /ˈfɔrtʃənətli/
  happily /ˈhæpili/
  helpfully /helpfəli/
  helplessly /helplisli/
  honestly /ˈanistli/
  hopefully /houpfəli/
  hopelessly /houplisli/
  originally /əˈridʒənəli/
  politely /pəˈlaitli/
  possibly /ˈpasəbli/
  usefully /ˈyusfəli/
  uselessly /ˈyuslisli/

Word formation: prefixes

We can often add the prefixes **un-**, **in-**, **im-**, **dis-**, **il-**, **in-** and **ir-** to adjectives to make new adjectives which mean the opposite.

Adjective	Opposite adjective
happy	→ **un**happy
visible	→ **in**visible
possible	→ **im**possible
obedient	→ **dis**obedient
logical	→ **il**logical
correct	→ **in**correct
regular	→ **ir**regular

Many adjectives beginning with **l** take the prefix **il-**, many beginning with **r** take the prefix **ir-** and many beginning with a vowel sound take the prefix **dis-**. However, there are many exceptions, so you will have to learn these as you find them.

Word formation: suffixes

We can often add the suffixes **-ee**, **-er**, **-ation**, **-ion**, and **-ment** to verbs to make related nouns.

Verb	Related nouns	
employ	→ employ**er**	(a person who provides work)
	→ employ**ee**	(a person who works)
	→ employ**ment**	(a job)
collect	→ collect**ion**	
inform	→ inform**ation**	

We can often add the suffixes **-ness** and **-ility** to adjectives to make related nouns.

Adjective	Related noun
dark	→ dark**ness**
happy	→ happi**ness**
possible	→ possib**ility**

We can often add the suffixes **-al**, **-ish**, **-ese** and **-ian** to nouns to make related adjectives.

Noun	Related adjective
origin	→ origin**al**
Pole	→ Pol**ish**
China	→ Chin**ese**
Egypt	→ Egypt**ian**

These rules are only guidelines. There are many exceptions, so you will have to learn these as you find them.

We can also use other suffixes to express general ideas:
1 Nouns ending in **-ism** often refer to abstract ideas: material**ism**, commun**ism**, capital**ism**.
2 Nouns ending in **-ist** often describe people and ideas: material**ist**, commun**ist**, capital**ist**.
3 Nouns ending in **-er** (or **-or**) often refer to occupations: employ**er**, football**er**, wait**er**, act**or**, conduct**or**
4 Nouns ending in **-ess** refer to females: wait**ress**, lion**ess**, act**ress**
5 Adjectives ending in **-ful** usually express the idea of being "full of": hope**ful**, beauti**ful**, faith**ful**
6 Adjectives ending in **-less** usually express the idea of being "without": hope**less**, penni**less**, use**less**

We call these related verbs, nouns, adjectives and adverbs "word families".

OXFORD
UNIVERSITY PRESS

Diana Pye

Star Team

Workbook

3

Let's remember!

Grammar

Irregular verbs: simple past

1 Complete the conversation.

Tara Did you go (you / go) to the movies yesterday afternoon, Joe?

Joe Yes, I did. (1) _____ (I / go) with Emma and Billy.

Tara What (2) _____ (you / see)?

Joe (3) _____ (we / see) a science fiction movie called Al.

(4) _____ (you / stay) at home yesterday?

Tara No, I didn't. (5) _____ (I / meet) your sister in town and

(6) _____ (we / go) shopping together.

Joe (7) _____ (she / spend) a lot of money?

Tara Yes, (8) _____ (she / do).

(9) _____ (she / buy) a lot of clothes.

Joe What other things

(10) _____ (she / buy)?

Tara (11) _____ (she / not buy) anything else.

Joe You mean, (12) _____ (she / not get) my birthday present!

Tara No, she didn't. (13) _____ (she / forget)!

Past continuous

2 What were they doing at five o'clock yesterday? Complete the questions and answers.

Was she doing her homework at 5pm? (do)

No, she wasn't. She was swimming. (swim)

1 ____ he _____ a movie on TV at 5pm? (watch)

No, he _____ . He _____ the guitar at 5pm. (play)

2 ____ they _____ cola at 5pm? (drink)

No, they _____ . They _____ hamburgers. (eat)

3 ____ the dog _____ in the park at 5pm? (run)

No, it _____ . It _____ in the kitchen. (sleep)

4 ____ she _____ a cake at 5pm? (make)

No, she _____ . She _____ in the yard. (read)

Simple past with ago

3 Rearrange the words to make sentences.

The / two hours / test / math / ago. / started

The math test started two hours ago.

1 left / The boys / half an hour / house / ago. / the

　_____

2 met / She / two weeks / her / ago. / boyfriend

　_____

3 months / Canada / ago. / two / visited / We

　_____

4 ago. / arrived / I / the restaurant / at / an hour

　_____

Simple past and past continuous

4 Complete the newspaper article. Use the simple past (4 verbs) and the past continuous (4 verbs).

Frank finds a new friend

Jim Jenkins is responsible for the chimpanzees at San Diego Zoo. While Jim was giving (give) the chimpanzees their food on Saturday morning, one of the animals opened (open) the door and (1) _____ (go) outside. There were a lot of people outside so the chimpanzee (2) _____ (run) down the street and into the park. A young boy called Frank (3) _____ (read) a book in the park. He (4) _____ (lie) in the sun and he (5) _____ (eat) some chocolate. The chimpanzee (6) _____ (sit) down next to him. Frank was very happy to see the chimpanzee and he (7) _____ (give) it some chocolate. When Mr. Jenkins arrived, Frank and the chimp (8) _____ (play) together!

Comparative and superlative adjectives

5 Compare three boxers. Write sentences with a comparative adjective and *than*.

Name	Age	Weight	Wins
Don	24	200lbs	16
Sam	21	210lbs	9
Jake	26	190lbs	31

Sam / young / Jake

Sam is younger than Jake.

1 Jake / old / Don .

　_____.

2 Sam / heavy / Jake

　_____.

3 Jake / good / Sam

　_____.

6 Now use *not as ... as*.

Jake is not as young as Sam.

1 Don _____ Jake.

2 Jake _____ Sam.

3 Sam _____ Jake.

7 Write sentences about the boxers. Use the superlative form of the adjectives.

~~old~~　good　young　heavy

Jake is the oldest.

1 _____.

2 _____.

3 _____.

will and going to

8 Choose and underline the correct form of the verb.

A I'll / *'m going to* buy some clothes now. Do you want to come with me?
B No, thanks. I*'ll* / 'm going to see you later.

1 A I'm hungry.
B I'll / 'm going to get you a sandwich.
2 A I've forgotten my book.
B Here, I'm going to / 'll lend you mine.
3 A What *will you* / *are you going to* do on Saturday evening?
4 B I don't know yet. Perhaps I'll / 'm going to watch a video.
5 A *Will you* / *Are you going to* play soccer this afternoon?
6 B No, we'll / 're going to see the New York Yankees play.
7 A Would you like coffee or tea?
B I'll / 'm going to have tea, please.
8 A Look at those black clouds! I'm sure it'll / 's going to rain.
B Let's run!

9 Match the sentences (1–5) with the uses of *will* and *going to* (a–e).

1 You look tired. I'll make the dinner. d
2 We're going to stay in a hotel by the ocean. __
3 Do you want an ice-cream cone? No, I'll just have a drink. __
4 Look! Fantastic! He's going to score a goal! __
5 In the future, there'll be computers in every home. __

a) a prediction about the future
b) a plan or intention
c) an instant decision
d) an offer of help
e) a prediction about something you can see or hear

Present perfect (affirmative and negative)

10 Complete the sentences.

She's made an enormous pizza. (make)
I haven't seen my boyfriend this week. (not see)

1 We _____ to Australia. (not go)
2 He _____ the President. (meet)
3 They _____ a lot of CDs. (buy)
4 She _____ a lot of money. (save)
5 He _____ that book. (not read)

Present perfect (question forms) with *ever*

11 Write questions with *ever*. Then write short answers.

you / go to Paris? ✗
Have you ever been to Paris?
No, I haven't.

1 they / eat Chinese food? ✓
_____?
_____.

2 they / play golf? ✗
_____?
_____.

3 he / met a famous baseball player ✓
_____?
_____.

4 you / climb a mountain? ✗
_____?
_____.

Vocabulary

Transportation

1 Match the definitions with the words in the box.

| motorcycle | ~~bicycle~~ | train |
| boat | truck | plane |

It has two wheels. It is very clean.
bicycle

1 It flies. It carries a lot of people.
_____

2 It has two wheels. It is very fast.
_____

3 It is very big and it travels on the road.
_____

4 It is very long and it travels on land.
_____

5 It travels on water. _____

Buildings

2 Read the sentences in order and complete the map of the town.

The museum (1) is opposite the hotel.
The library (2) is between the hotel and the bank (3).
The parking lot (4) is behind the library.
The book store (5) is opposite the bank.
The church (6) is opposite the post office (7).
The church isn't next to the book store.

At the restaurant

3 Complete the conversations. Use the words in the box.

| wine   melon   soup   main course |
| chicken salad   ice cream   ~~appetizer~~ |

Waiter Would you like an appetizer, madam?

Woman Yes. For my appetizer, I'll have a slice of (1) _____ , please. Then for the main course, I'd like the (2) _____ . And for dessert, I'll have an (3) _____ .

Waiter What would you like, sir?

Man For my appetizer, I'll have a bowl of (4) _____ . Then for the (5) _____ , I'll have roast beef.

Waiter What would you like to drink?

Man We'll have a bottle of (6) _____ , please.

Describing people: personality

4 Complete the sentences. Use the words in the box.

| modest   vain   shy   ~~cheerful~~   generous |

Sara's always smiling and laughing. She's cheerful.

1 Ed's nice but very quiet.

He's _____ .

2 Pete's very smart but he never talks about himself.

He's _____ .

3 Katie shares her things with other people.

She's _____ .

4 Clare always talks about how wonderful she is.

She's _____ .

Skills work

Life after school

1 Complete the sentences. Use *Alison* or *Tim*.

Life after school –
Alison

1 I'm in my last year at high school here in Boston and I'm studying math and
5 Spanish. Most of my friends are going to go to college next September, but I don't want to go this year. I enjoy studying but I'd like to take a year off and travel around the
10 world. I especially want to go to South America. I've never been there and it would be a fantastic opportunity to practice my Spanish. I definitely want to go to college but I haven't decided what
15 subjects I'll study. I hope I'll have a better idea when I get back from my travels next year!

Life after school –
Tim

20 My favorite subjects at school are Latin and Greek. I'd like to continue studying them when I leave
25 next summer, but my parents want me to choose more useful subjects. They say I'll never get a job if I study ancient Greek and I think they're probably right! I'd like to become a journalist when I finish college,
30 so I've decided I'll study English or geography. Before I go to college in September, I'm going to find a job for the summer here in New York. I want to earn money and have a beach vacation on the
35 Caribbean.

Alison is studying in Boston.

1 _____ wants to travel for a year.

2 _____ would like to study Latin and Greek.

3 _____ wants to practice Spanish.

4 _____ wants to be a journalist.

5 _____ is going to college in September.

6 _____ hasn't decided what to study at college.

7 _____ will decide what to study next year.

8 _____ is going to work in the summer.

2 Find words or phrases in the text with these meanings.

final (line 1) *last*

1 like (line 8) _____

2 great (line 12) _____

3 return (line 16) _____

4 work (line 27) _____

5 very old (line 27) _____

3 Study the notes. Then, complete the text about life after school.

What I'm doing now	studying art and history at school in Osaka
What I'd like to do after school	take a year off
Why?	travel around the world
What I don't want to do	go straight to college
Why?	to practice my English
What I'd like to do in the future	become an architect

Right now, I'm *studying art and history at school in Osaka*. After school, I'd like to (1) _____ because

(2) _____.

I don't want to (3) _____

because (4) _____.

In the future, I'd like to

(5) _____.

7

Puzzles

1 Find and circle the kinds of transportation.

(train, helicopter, boat, truck, van, bus, scooter, motorcycle, bicycle, plane, tram)

2 Where do you find these objects? Label the pictures with the words in the box.

bank   church   movie theater   ~~library~~
post office   train station   grocery store

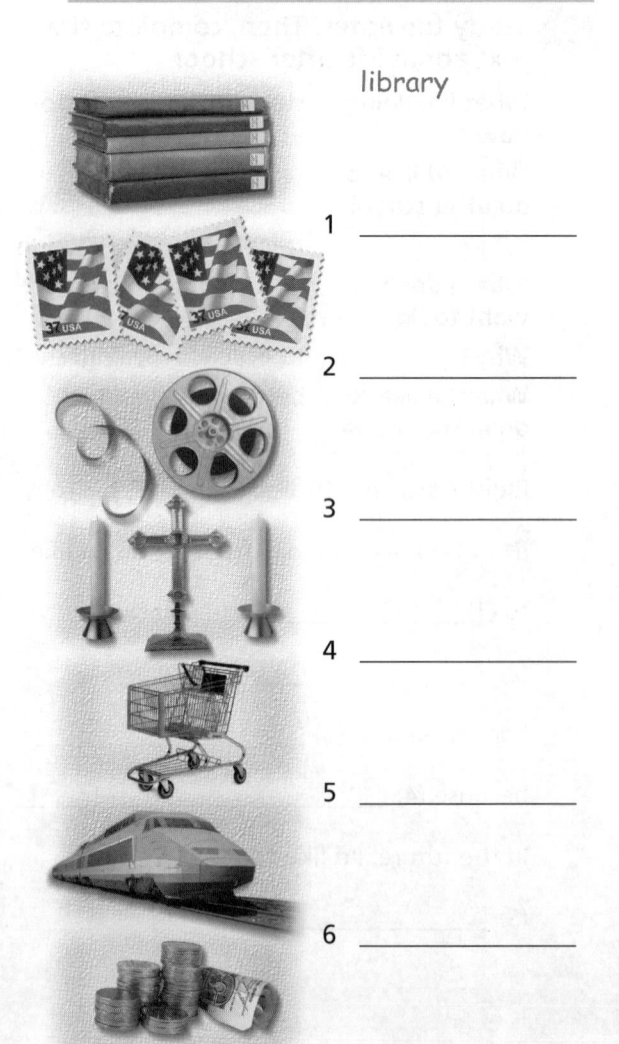

library
1 _____
2 _____
3 _____
4 _____
5 _____
6 _____

3 Complete the puzzle.

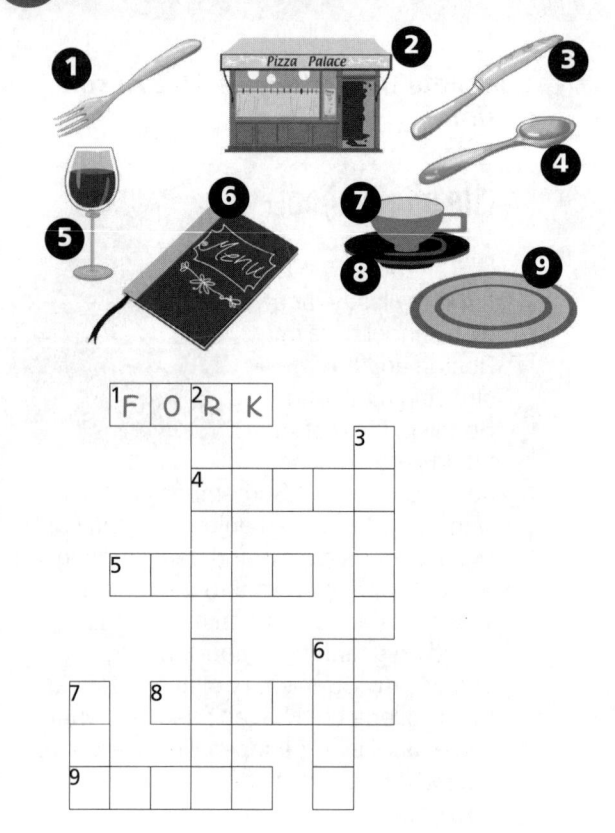

1 F O 2R K

4 Write the names of the objects.

g a l i d t i m a r a c e
digital camera

1 c u s b r i l o a n
_____

2 p o l t a p t o r u p e c m
_____ _____

3 l c l e e h n o p
_____ _____

4 t e t c a s s e y a p r l e
_____ _____

5 p c e r o n i h m o
_____

1 New York, New York!

1 Read the conversation. Then complete the sentences. Use *Tom*, *Jet*, or *Meg*.

It's early evening and Jet and Tom are waiting for Meg in Central Park.

Jet Has Meg ever been to the park before?

Tom No, never. Oh, look! There she is. Hi, Meg! Over here!

Meg Hi! Sorry I'm late. I took a wrong turn and I got lost!

Tom Would you like a drink now? It's on me.

Meg Yes, please, I would.

Tom Let's go to that place which is near the lake.

Jet Can I carry your bag, Meg?

Meg No. I'm OK, thanks. It isn't heavy. Whose are those?

Tom They're Jet's. He goes everywhere on his in-line skates.

Meg Cool! Guess what? I saw another movie star this morning! That's two in one week!

Jet Who did you see?

Meg The woman who was in *The Hours*. I'm sure it was her.

Tom Nicole Kidman! You're joking! She's the most beautiful person I've ever seen!

Tom and Jet are in Central Park.

1 Tom and Jet are waiting for _____.

2 _____ is late.

3 _____ offers to buy Meg a drink.

4 The in-line skates belong to _____.

5 _____ saw a movie star this morning.

Communication

Possession: *whose?*

2 Complete the conversations.

A Whose in-line skates are those?
B They're Eve's.
A Whose bike is that?
B It's my sister's.

1 **A** _____ magazines _____?
   B _____ my mom's.

2 **A** _____ computer _____?
   B _____ our parents'.

3 **A** _____ limousine _____?
   B _____ Leonardo's.

Offers and replies

3 Write conversations. Use *Can I …* or *Would you like …* and the sentences in the box.

> No thanks. I wouldn't.
> No. I'm OK thanks.   Sure! Thanks.
> Yes please. I would.

I / buy you a drink? ✗
A Can I buy you a drink?
B No. I'm OK thanks.

you / a drink? ✓
A Would you like a drink?
B Yes please, I would.

1 I / get you some cookies? ✓
   A _____?
   B _____.

2 you / a sandwich? ✗
   A _____?
   B _____.

1

Grammar

Simple past

1 Complete the sentences.

Last week we *attended* (attend) a talk about jobs. Different people (1) _____ (come) and (2) _____ (talk) about their jobs. A woman who creates computer software (3) _____ (show) us some great games. My friend Luke (4) _____ (ask), (5) "_____ (you create) any of the games?" "No," she (6) _____ (tell) Luke. "I (7) _____ (not make) any of these games. But I have made many others." Luke (8) _____ (say), "I'd like to do that job because I don't want to go to college." He asked, "How (9) _____ (you learn) to make games?" "I (10) _____ (go) to college for three years!" said the woman.

Present perfect

2 Write questions and answers. Use short forms.

they / visit Seattle? (San Francisco / twice)
Have they ever visited Seattle?
No, they haven't. But they've visited San Francisco twice.

1 he / break his leg? (his nose)

   _____?
   _____
   _____.

2 you / eat / dolphin meat? (whale meat)

   _____?
   _____
   _____.

3 she / meet / your dad? (my mom)

   _____?
   _____
   _____.

4 you and Bill / give / a talk in Spanish? (a talk in French)

   _____?
   _____
   _____.

3 Write five true sentences about your experiences. Use some of the verbs in the box.

| use   be   eat   not meet   see   not visit |

I've used a laptop computer.

1 _____.
2 _____.
3 _____.
4 _____.
5 _____.

Simple past and present perfect

4 Complete the rules. Use the simple past or the present perfect.

1 We use _____ to refer to a specific time in the past.

2 We use _____ to talk about experiences and to connect the past to the present.

10

5 Complete Kelly's letter.

Apartment 14
Central Park Avenue
New York
December 15 2006

Dear Keiko,

I *arrived* (arrive) in New York last Wednesday and I *haven't stopped* (not stop) since then! I'm staying with my aunt. She (1) _____ (take) me to see a lot of places in the last three days. Yesterday we (2) _____ (visit) the Guggenheim Museum. I (3) _____ (never see) such an enormous museum! It (4) _____ (be) an exhausting day!

The day before yesterday, we (5) _____ (see) a musical on Broadway. My aunt thinks it's fantastic and she (6) _____ (go) to see it six times! I'm afraid I (7) _____ (not think) it was very good but I (8) _____ (not tell) her!

The only thing I don't like are the evenings. We (9) _____ (not go) to a club once and I (10) _____ (not meet) anyone my own age. But my aunt is 82 so it's not surprising!

Love from,
Kelly

Relative pronouns *who* and *which / that*

6 Study the definitions. Then, complete the rules.

A microwave oven is a machine which / that cooks things quickly.

A journalist is a person who writes newspaper articles.

A whale is an animal which / that lives in the ocean.

1 We use the relative pronoun *who* for _____ .

2 We use the relative pronoun *which* or *that* for _____ or _____ .

7 Complete the definitions. Use *who* or *which / that*.

A Ferrari is a car *which* costs a lot of money.
1 A vet is a person _____ works with animals.
2 A dishwasher is a machine _____ washes dishes.
3 A sound engineer is a person _____ records music.
4 Kangaroos are animals _____ only live in Australia.

8 Write definitions.

a watch / machine / tells the time

A watch is a machine which tells the time.

1 a mechanic / person / works in a garage

_____.

2 *Nike* / company / makes sneakers

_____.

3 a space shuttle / machine / travels into space

_____.

4 cats / animals / sleep a lot

_____.

5 e-mail / technology / uses the Internet

_____.

2 My kind of town.

1 Read the text about Los Angeles. Then, choose and write the correct topic for each paragraph. Use the topics in the box.

> The beach scene   A cultural center   Something for everyone
> America's second biggest city   A multi-cultural city   A glamorous reputation

Glamour capital of the USA

1 _____

Los Angeles, on the United States west coast, is one of the most exciting cities in the world. With around 3.8 million inhabitants, it is the second biggest city in the United States.

2 _____

LA has built its reputation on the glamor of the movie industry in nearby Hollywood. On the Hollywood Mile pavement there are over 2,000 pink stars with the names of famous movie stars. Beverly Hills, with its fabulous houses and expensive stores, is home to the rich and famous.

3 _____

Nearly half the population of LA came originally from Latin America. There are also many Asian residents, including Japanese and nearly half a million Chinese people. This creates a fantastic mix of different languages, cultures, fashions, and foods.

4 _____

LA is famous for its theme parks like *Universal City* and *Disneyland*. But it is an important cultural center as well. It has 80 theaters and nearly 300 museums and art galleries. The most important is the *Getty Center* which has one of the world's most expensive art collections.

5 _____

LA has some fantastic beaches. Some, such as Malibu, are world-famous because they are the location for well-known movies or TV series. Others are great for surfing and attract fashionable young people.

6 _____

So – whether you are a surfer looking for excitement, a movie fan hoping to meet a star, or an actor looking for a place to live – you will find that there is something for everyone in the glamor capital of the USA.

2 Read the text again. Then, write answers.

1 How many people live in Los Angeles?
   _____.

2 Where do the rich and famous live?
   _____.

3 Where do half of the population of LA come from?
   _____.

4 What is in the *Getty Center*?
   _____.

3 Find words or phrases in the text with these meanings.

approximately (paragraph 1) around

1 more than (paragraph 2) _____
2 well-known (paragraph 2) _____
3 almost (paragraph 3) _____
4 a lot of (paragraph 3) _____
5 too (paragraph 4) _____
6 wonderful (paragraph 5) _____
7 a person who likes movies (paragraph 6) _____

12

Vocabulary

British English and American English

1 Find and write the American English words.

fall   3 _____   6 _____
1 _____   4 _____   7 _____
2 _____   5 _____

2 Write labels for the pictures. Use the British English words in the box.

| biscuits lift ~~taxi~~ crisps underground petrol sweets |

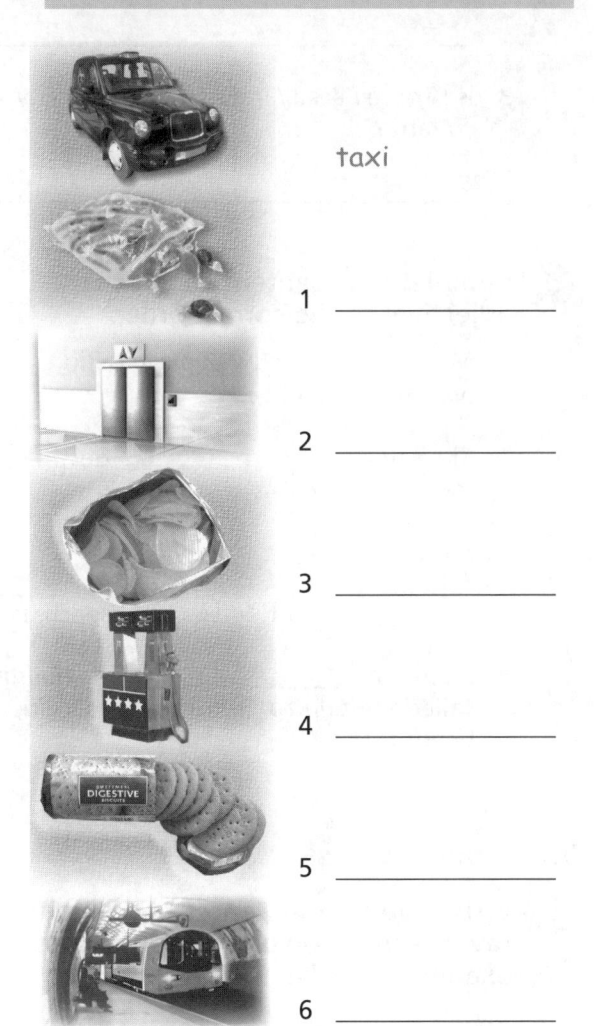

taxi
1 _____
2 _____
3 _____
4 _____
5 _____
6 _____

3 Write the British English words.

fall   autumn
1 freeway   _____
2 movie   _____
3 apartment   _____
4 gas   _____
5 vacation   _____
6 chips   _____
7 candy   _____
8 subway   _____
9 sidewalk   _____
10 movie theater _____

4 Choose and circle the British English words.

color   theatre   favourite   center   colour   theater   favorite   centre

5 Change the American English words to British English words.

Buddy and I live in the center *centre* of town. His (1) *apartment*'s _____ on the (2) *first floor* _____ and mine's on the (3) *second floor* _____. There isn't (4) an *elevator* _____ so we have to use the stairs. I don't have a car so I usually take the (5) *subway* _____ to work. When I'm late, I call a (6) *cab* _____. In the evening, I often go to the (7) *movie theater* _____. Western (8) *movies* _____ are my (9) *favorite* _____.

13

2

Writing

Writing about places

1 Write the adjectives in the correct lists.

~~attractive~~ ~~dark~~ new large black tourist beautiful old glass awful modern small white

Quality	Size	Age
attractive	tiny	ancient
famous	tall	historical
(1) _____	(3) _____	(5) _____
(2) _____	(4) _____	(6) _____
		(7) _____

Color	Material	Type
dark	stone	beach
gray	(10) _____	vacation
(8) _____		(11) _____
(9) _____		

2 Write sentences.

Lijiang is a town in the south west of China. (historical)

Lijiang is a historical town in the south west of China.

1 The town is on a canal. (beautiful)

   _____ .

2 Lijiang is a tourist destination. (popular)

   _____ .

Building sentences

3 Lijiang has a lot of buildings. (beautiful, old)

   _____ .

4 There are some mountains near Lijiang. (famous)

   _____ .

3 Rearrange the words to make sentences. Put the adjectives in the correct order (quality, size, age, color, material, type).

building / an / in Buenos Aires. / is / old / The Colón Theater / attractive

The Colón Theater is an attractive, old building in Buenos Aires.

1 famous / Plaza de Mayo / a / square. / big / is

   _____

2 tourist / The Metropolitan Cathedral / popular / attraction. / is / a

   _____

3 is / There / area / industrial / in the city. / a / large

   _____

4 Complete the sentences. Put the adjectives in the correct order.

My *favorite vacation* place is Rio. (vacation, favorite)

1 Rio is a _____ _____ destination. (popular, tourist)

2 It is an _____ , _____ , _____ resort. (attractive, beach, large)

3 Rio has a _____ , _____ building called the *Centro Cultural Banco*. (old, beautiful)

Your writing task

5 Write five true sentences about your favorite vacation place. Include some examples of adjectives + noun.

My favorite vacation place is …

14

Units 1–2

Progress check

Grammar

1 Complete the conversation. Use the simple past or the present perfect.

A (1) _____ (you ever visit) an English-speaking country?

B Yes. (2) _____ (I be) to the USA twice.

A When (3) _____ (you go)?

B (4) _____ (I go) there two years ago. And you?

A (5) _____ (I never go) to the USA but (6) _____ (I visit) Canada. (7) _____ (I spend) last summer there.

B (8) _____ (you stay) long in Vancouver?

A No, I didn't. (9) _____ (I not have) time.

2 Complete the definitions. Use *who*, *whose*, or *which / that*.

1 A waitress is a woman _____ works in a restaurant.

2 A camera is a machine _____ takes photographs.

3 Mark Twain was a writer _____ books include *The Adventures of Tom Sawyer*.

4 A kangaroo is an animal _____ only lives in Australia.

5 An elevator is a machine _____ carries people up and down.

6 A tweenager is a person _____ is between ten and thirteen years old.

Vocabulary

3 Complete the chart.

British English	American English
biscuits	(1) _____
pavement	(2) _____
(3) _____	chips
(4) _____	cab
queue	(5) _____
sweets	(6) _____
shop	(7) _____
(8) _____	elevator
(9) _____	movies
holiday	(10) _____
petrol	(11) _____

Communication

4 Complete the conversations. Use the words in the box.

| Would They're I would my friends' |
| Can I Whose |

1 A _____ apartment is this?

B It's _____.

2 A _____ get you a drink?

B Thanks. Yes.

3 A _____ you like a cookie?

B Yes please, _____.

4 A Whose DVDs are those?

B _____ my brother's.

15

Units 1-2
Graded exercises

1 Complete Jane's e-mail to her best friend. Use the simple past.

To: sue.harris@metoo.com
From: jane.richards@spacenet.com
Date: July 16 2006
Subject: vacation

Hi Sue!

Well, it's vacation time at last! I'm having a fantastic time this week. Yesterday, I *stayed* (stay) in bed until 11am.
I (1) _____ (watch) TV all afternoon, then I (2) _____ (go) to a party until midnight!

On Saturday, I (3) _____ (buy) a new swimsuit but I (4) _____ (not go) swimming because the weather (5) _____ (be) awful. Instead, I (6) _____ (meet) a friend and we (7) _____ (spend) the afternoon playing computer games.

My brother Clive (8) _____ (start) his vacation job on Monday. He's a waiter in a café. I (9) _____ (take) my friends there on Tuesday. Clive (10) _____ (not like) that. He (11) _____ (not speak) to us so we (12) _____ (not stay)!

Write back soon with all your news!

Bye for now,

Jane

2 Complete the conversation. Use the simple past or the present perfect.

A ever go / the theater?
  Have you ever been to the theater?
B Yes, I have.
A see / any plays by Shakespeare?
  (1) _____?
B Yes, I have.
A Which plays / you / see?
  (2) _____?
B I / see / *Hamlet* and *Macbeth*
  (3) _____.

A Where / you / see / them?
  (4) _____?
B In New York. And you? see / any plays by Shakespeare?
  (5) _____?
A No, never.

3 Write definitions.

A pilot is a person who flies a plane.

Franz Kafka was a writer whose books include *Metamorphosis*.

A microwave oven is a machine which / that cooks food.

1 A doctor _____.

2 Aldous Huxley _____.

3 A digital camera _____.

4 Dinosaurs _____.

5 A waiter _____.

3 An American deli.

1 Read the conversation. Are the sentences true or false?

The friends are meeting again at their favorite deli.

Bud How do you like New York, Meg?
Meg It's fantastic. Everyone's so friendly.
Bud Has Tom shown you the sights yet?
Meg We've already been to a lot of places in the last month, but I haven't visited the Statue of Liberty yet.
Bud Would you like to go with me? How about Saturday?
Meg I'd love to, but I'd rather go on Sunday.
Bella Hi! I'm sorry I'm late. I've just finished my gym class.
Meg Let's have an ice-cream cone. They're on me.
Bud I'd prefer a juice, please.

Meg has been in New York for a month.
True

1 Meg has already visited the Statue of Liberty. _____

2 Bud invites Meg to go with him on Saturday. _____

3 Bella has just come from her gym class. _____

4 Meg offers to buy them ice-cream cones. _____

Communication

Preferences

2 Complete the conversations. Use *I'd prefer* or *I'd rather*.

   A Would you like some juice?
   B No thanks. I'd prefer a cola.

1 **A** Would you like to have lunch at one?
   B No. _____ have lunch now.

2 **A** Would you like some pasta?
   B No. _____ a steak.

3 **A** Would you like to watch a video?
   B No. _____ to go out.

4 **A** Would you like to come with me?
   B No. _____ go alone!

Apologies

3 Complete the conversations. Use the phrases in the box.

really sorry   ~~sorry~~   apologize

   A That's my pen!
   B Oh, I'm very sorry.

1 **A** Hey! Don't do that!
   B I _____ .

2 **A** You've taken my magazine!
   B I'm _____ .

3 **A** I was using that pen!
   B I _____ .

3

Grammar

Present perfect with *for* and *since*

1 Complete the rules. Use *a period of time* or *a point in time*.

1 We use *for* with _____.

2 We use *since* with _____.

2 Complete the time expressions. Use *for* or *since*.

since Sunday
for two hours

1 _____ last year
2 _____ a few months
3 _____ last Wednesday
4 _____ weeks and weeks
5 _____ the summer
6 _____ the past two days
7 _____ 2004
8 _____ a long time
9 _____ six o'clock
10 _____ ten years

3 Write sentences. Use *for* or *since*.

I / have / my scooter / two months
I've had my scooter for two months.

1 He / play / on the team / a year
   _____.

2 She / not see / her sister / the summer vacation
   _____.

3 We / win / two games / John became captain
   _____.

4 They / be / good friends / a long time
   _____.

4 Write true answers. Use *for* or *since*.

1 How long have you studied English?
   I've studied English for/since _____.

2 How long have you been at your school?
   _____.

3 How long have you known your best friend?
   _____.

4 How long has your family lived here?
   _____.

Present perfect with *just*, *already*, *yet*

5 Write sentences about the pictures. Use *just*.

He / break / a glass
He has just broken a glass.

1 she / finish / her lunch
   _____.

2 he / become / captain
   _____.

3 she / win / the race
   _____.

6
Write two sentences about the people in the pictures. Use *already* and *yet*.

He / buy / a ticket
He has already bought a ticket.
He / see / the movie
He hasn't seen the movie yet.

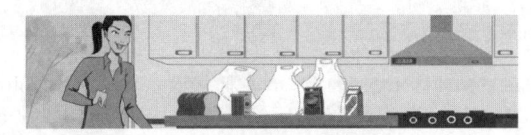

1 She / do / the shopping
_____ .

She / not make / the sandwiches
_____ .

2 He / change / his clothes
_____ .

He / not brush / his hair
_____ .

3 They / start / the game
_____ .

They / not score / any goals
_____ .

4 He / clean / his room
_____ .

He / not make / his bed
_____ .

7
Oscar and Martine are preparing for a party. Complete the conversation with *already* or *yet*.

Martine Have you bought the drinks yet?

Oscar No, but I've (1) _____ prepared the food.

Martine And have you organized the music (2) _____?

Oscar I haven't chosen the CDs (3) _____ but I've (4) _____ checked the equipment.

Martine And have you cleaned the kitchen (5) _____?

Oscar No, I haven't! And you? What have you done?

Martine I haven't done anything (6) _____!

Adverbs of manner

8
Are the underlined words *adjectives* or *adverbs*?

He can run very <u>fast</u>.   adverb
He's a <u>fast</u> runner.   adjective

1 He is a <u>hard</u> worker. _____
2 He works <u>hard</u>. _____
3 I don't play chess <u>well</u>. _____
4 I'm a <u>good</u> player. _____
5 The story ends <u>happily</u>. _____
6 The story has a <u>happy</u> ending. _____

9
Complete the sentences about you, your friend, and your family. Use adverbs.

1 I don't sing _____ .
2 My friend speaks English _____ .
3 My mother drives _____ .

4 Famous Americans.

1 Read the biography of Abraham Lincoln. Then, choose and write the correct topic for each paragraph.

> The American Civil War   A very great man   A poor childhood
> Freeing the slaves   A world of injustice

Abraham Lincoln – an American hero

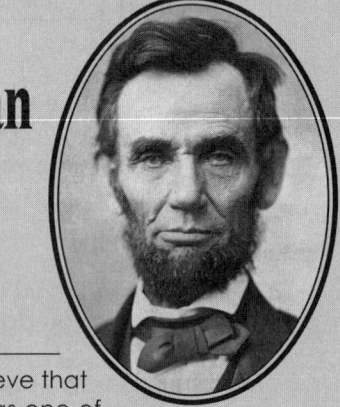

1 _____

Most Americans believe that Abraham Lincoln was one of their greatest presidents. But the sixteenth President of the United States of America came from a poor home. He was born in 1809 on a small farm in Kentucky. As a child, young Abraham didn't go to school. He studied hard at home and eventually he went to college and became a lawyer.

2 _____

Lincoln grew up in a society of injustice and discrimination. In the southern states of the Union, all black people were slaves. These people suffered terrible injustice from the white people who bought and sold them. But attitudes were changing in the north and many people wanted to free the black slaves.

3 _____

Abraham Lincoln became President of the United States in 1860. He was opposed to slavery. Immediately after his election, the Civil War between the northern and southern states started. It lasted four years and many people died. Lincoln was a great leader and he changed American history when he led the northern states to victory.

4 _____

His other great achievement was the abolition of slavery. On January 1 1863, he signed the Emancipation Proclamation which declared slavery to be illegal. Millions of black people became free. But they did not win the same rights as white people until a hundred years later.

5 _____

On April 14 1865, only five days after the end of the war, Lincoln was at a theater in Washington DC when an actor shot him. He later died in hospital. Today, the people of the USA see Abraham Lincoln as a great national hero.

2 Find these pronouns in the text. What do they refer to?

He (line 5) Abraham Lincoln

1 them (line 14) _____

2 It (line 21) _____

3 they (line 28) _____

4 He (line 32) _____

3 Read the text again and correct the mistake in each sentence.

Abraham Lincoln was born on a **big** farm.

Abraham Lincoln was born on a **small** farm.

1 In the **northern** states of the Union, all black people were slaves.

_____

_____.

2 The Civil War lasted **five** years.

_____

_____.

3 On April 14 1865, only five days **before** the end of the war, …

_____

_____.

20

Vocabulary

Feelings and emotions

1 Find eight adjectives.

```
H S A A V E J S O
C O N F I D E N T
H D G I L M A X Y
A F R A I D L U S
P R Y E M W O B R
P E N V I O U S T
Y S T U P D S F R
L A T P R O U D M
R D J H A F E C U
```

2 Write the nouns.

fciencodne   confidence

1 nyev   _____
2 esalyujo   _____
3 ganre   _____
4 sesdasn   _____
5 ispanshpe   _____
6 epdir   _____
7 afre   _____

3 Complete Isabel's letter to her best friend. Use the words in the box.

afraid   angry   confident   envious   happy   ~~proud~~

Hotel Pacific
Auckland
New Zealand
April 7 2005

Dear Elsa,

Guess what? I've been bungee jumping! I'm so proud of myself! Before the jump, I didn't feel at all (1) _____ . In fact, I was really (2) _____ . It was a fantastic feeling, but I was (3) _____ to be back on the ground!

My brother's really (4) _____ . He wanted to jump but he's too young. My dad was (5) _____ when I told him. He says it's very dangerous. But it's too late now!

Love,

Isabel

4 Write true, short answers.

1 What makes you feel happy?

   _____.

2 Have you ever felt jealous?

   _____.

3 What are you afraid of?

   _____.

4 When was the last time you felt angry with someone?

   _____.

4 Writing

Building paragraphs

Writing about movies and books

1 Read the model paragraph. Then, choose and circle the correct topic (A–D).

A The characters
B Why this is my favorite book
C The story
D The author

MODEL PARAGRAPH

My favorite book is *The Hound of the Baskervilles*. The story is about the terrible secret of the Baskerville family. A strange dog kills Sir Charles Baskerville near his country house. The local people are very scared and they call this terrible dog the Hound of the Baskervilles. They believe that the animal will kill again. Sir Charles's nephew does not believe the story of the strange dog. He asks the world-famous detective, Sherlock Holmes, to discover who really killed his uncle. The story is exciting, dramatic, and very scary.

2 Study the notes for another paragraph. Then, choose and write the correct topic from the list (A–D) in exercise 1.

Topic: _____

creator of world-famous detective, Sherlock Holmes
The Hound of the Baskervilles 1902
his longest, most famous book
Doyle born Scotland 1859
studied medicine, became a doctor
very popular writer, became "Sir" Arthur in 1902
died 1930

3 Complete the paragraph about the author of *The Hound of the Baskervilles*. Use the notes in exercise 2.

Sir Arthur Conan Doyle was the creator of world-famous detective, Sherlock Holmes. He wrote (1) _____.

It is (2) _____.

Conan Doyle (3) _____.

He (4) _____

and _____.

He (5) _____ and

_____.

He (6) _____.

Your writing task

4 Study the notes about the characters of the book. Then write a paragraph about them.

Main character: Sherlock Holmes
famous detective
address: 221b Baker Street, London
world's best detective, only investigates very strange events, such as the secret of the Baskervilles
very smart, sees things that other people can't see, always studies facts and small details
always succeeds

Other important character: Doctor Watson
Holmes's faithful friend & partner
admires Holmes very much
helps Holmes with all his investigations
helps him discover the Baskerville secret

The main character in the book is Sherlock Holmes ...

Progress check

Grammar

1 Complete the sentences. Use *for* or *since*.

1 I've lived here _____ three months.
2 We've been good friends _____ 1999.
3 She's studied English _____ four years.
4 He's had extra classes _____ the past six weeks.
5 They've worked hard _____ eight o'clock this morning.
6 Have you been home _____ June?

2 Rearrange the words to make sentences.

1 finished / yet. / his tests / He / has not
   _____
2 your parents / met / Has / yet? / she
   _____
3 already / We / that movie. / seen / have
   _____
4 I / a new school. / started / just / have
   _____
5 ordered / yet. / our meal / have not / We
   _____

3 Complete the sentences. Change the adjectives to adverbs.

1 He drives very _____. (fast)
2 They worked _____. (hard)
3 He answered _____. (polite)
4 She shouted _____. (angry)
5 We get up _____. (early)
6 The story ended _____. (tragic)

Vocabulary

4 Complete the chart.

Adjectives	Nouns
proud	(1)_____
(2)_____	envy
jealous	(3)_____
(4)_____	confidence
angry	(5)_____
happy	(6)_____
sad	(7)_____
(8)_____	fear

Communication

5 Complete the conversations. Use *I'd prefer* or *I'd rather*.

1 **A** Would you like to learn Spanish?
   B No. _____ to learn Italian.

2 **A** Would you like a piece of cake?
   B No thanks. _____ a sandwich.

3 **A** Would you like to go camping?
   B No. _____ stay at a hotel.

4 **A** Would you like to watch the soccer game?
   B No. _____ to see a movie.

Units 3-4

Graded exercises

1 Write the adverbs. Then complete the sentences.

bad — badly

a) beautiful _____
b) early _____
c) sudden _____
d) fast _____
e) rude _____
f) loud _____
g) hard _____
h) tragic _____
i) good _____

I can't understand his English because he speaks *badly*.

1 I arrived late because my scooter _____ stopped.

2 I don't like the story because it ends _____.

3 The teacher was angry because Tim interrupted her _____.

4 She speaks German very _____.

5 Her test scores are good because she worked really _____.

6 I always get up _____ on Mondays.

7 Lots of people come to her concerts because she sings _____.

8 He woke the baby up when he spoke _____.

9 He crashed into a tree because he was driving very _____.

2 Complete Rosy's e-mail. Use *for*, *since*, *just*, *already*, or *yet*.

To	liz.read@youandme.com
From:	rosy.dean@dreamnet.com
Date:	October 3 2006
Subject:	news from New York

Hello Liz,
How are things? Sorry I haven't written *for* a long time but I've been very busy (1) _____ August 1 when we came to live in New York. I've (2) _____ started my new school here. That was last week and I've (3) _____ made a new friend. Her name's Sara and she's (4) _____ come here too! My brother hasn't started college (5) _____ so he's still at home. My sister hasn't returned from Mexico (6) _____. She's been there (7) _____ nearly a month now. Mom's worried that she won't come back! We haven't had any news from her (8) _____ two weeks.
Have you given Joe my new address? I haven't heard from him (9) _____. I hope he hasn't (10) _____ forgotten me and found a new girlfriend!
Love,
Rosy

3 Write true sentences. Use the present perfect.

know (someone) / since

I've known my best friend since March.

1 already / study (something)

_____.

2 speak to (someone) / since

_____.

3 just / do (something)

_____.

4 already / finish (something)

_____.

5 not do (something) / yet

_____.

6 not see (someone) / since

_____.

5 On Broadway!

1 Read the conversation. Then, correct these false sentences.

It's Saturday night after the show on Broadway.

Tom What a show! You have to go to drama school, Jet. If you become a star, we'll have free tickets for your shows. Let's go for a coffee.

Jet Sorry, but I have to go home. I need to sleep.

Bella I have to go home, too. Dad will be angry if I get in late again.

Tom Well, that leaves you and me, Meg. Are you coming?

Meg OK, but I can't stay late. I'm visiting the Statue of Liberty tomorrow.

If Tom becomes a star, they'll have free tickets.

If Jet becomes a star, they'll have free tickets.

1 **Jet** wants to go for a coffee.

_____.

2 **Tom** needs to sleep.

_____.

3 Bella's **mom** will be angry if she is late.

_____.

4 **Bella** is visiting the Statue of Liberty tomorrow.

_____.

Communication

Obligation (*have to*, *need to*) and prohibition (*can't*)

2 Rearrange the words to make sentences.

make / You / a right / can't / here.
You can't make a right here.

1 have to / passport. / your / You / show

_____

2 wear / sports shoes / need to / You / in the gym.

_____

3 in the library. / can't / You / talk

_____

Obligation (*have to*) and lack of obligation (*don't have to*)

3 Complete the questions and answers.

A Do you have to do the dishes? ✓
B Yes I do. And I have to help in the yard!

A Do you have to do the dishes? ✗
B No I don't. But I have to clean my room.

1 A _____ make dinner? ✗
  B _____ help with the shopping.

2 A _____ take the dog out? ✓
  B _____ feed the cat.

Grammar

Zero conditional

1 Complete the sentences.

If you (eat) a lot of candy, you (get) bad teeth

If you eat a lot of candy, you get bad teeth.

1 If she (practice) sports, she (stay) fit

  If _____.

2 If I (help), Mom (give) me some money

  If _____.

3 If you (melt) ice, it (turn) into water

  If _____.

4 If the teacher (ask) a question, the students (put up) their hands

  If _____
  _____.

2 Complete the sentences.

(not feel / hungry before lunch)

If I have a big breakfast, I don't feel hungry before lunch.

1 (look / in a dictionary)

  If I don't understand a word in English,
  _____.

2 (not make / a noise)

  If I get home late at night,
  _____.

3 (buy / a lot of things)

  If I have a lot of money,
  _____.

First conditional

3 Write sentences.

If she (not work), she (not pass) her test

If she doesn't work hard, she won't pass her test.

1 If he (not hurry), he (miss) the train

  _____
  _____.

2 If it (rain) tomorrow, I (not go) out

  _____
  _____.

3 If you (not drive) carefully, a police officer (stop) you

  _____
  _____.

4 If they (not stop) eating, they (be) sick

  _____
  _____.

4 Complete the predictions.

If I save my pocket money,

I'll buy some CDs.

1 If you work very hard,

_____ .

2 If I pick some apples tomorrow,

_____ .

3 If they play well,

_____ .

4 If you eat all that ice cream,

_____ .

have to

5 Study the chart. It shows the Olympic pentathlon sports that athletes *have to* / *don't have to* do. Complete the sentences with *have to* or *don't have to*.

Olympic sports	Pentathlon events	
running (3000m)		✓
jumping		✗
gun shooting		✓
horse jumping		✓
tennis		✗
swimming (200m)		✓

Pentathlon athletes have to run 3000m.

1 They _____ jump.

2 They _____ shoot with a gun.

3 They _____ do horse jumping.

4 They _____ play tennis.

5 They _____ swim 200m.

can't, have to and need to

6 Complete the sentences. Use *can't*, *have to*, *don't have to* or *need to*.

Nurses need to understand a lot about health problems.

1 You _____ drive fast in the town.

2 You _____ clean your teeth after meals.

3 You _____ wash your hands after meals.

4 Bank clerks _____ know how to count.

5 She _____ travel if she doesn't have any money.

6 You _____ have a passport to go to a foreign country.

6 Welcome to Oz.

1 Read the text about Australia. Then, choose and write the correct topic for each paragraph.

> Aborigines today   A nation of sports people
> A multi-cultural society   Unique wildlife   A modern cultural nation

Life down under

1 _____

Modern Australia is a multi-cultural society. In the 1960s and 1970s large numbers of Italians and Greeks settled in Australia. Some people describe Australia's second biggest city, Melbourne, as the third largest Greek city in the world! More recently, many Asian immigrants have arrived in Australia and they are changing the cultural identity of society.

2 _____

For two centuries after the first white European settlers arrived in Australia, the Aborigines suffered terrible injustice. Thousands died and their culture nearly disappeared. Today there is still discrimination but things are changing. The Aborigines have the same rights as other Australians. They succeed in all areas of society.

3 _____

Sports are very important national activities and Australians are excellent at many sports. The most popular sports are cricket and Australian Rules football, a spectacular game unique to Australia. Australia's rugby team, the _Wallabies_, is one of the world's best. Australia's many great sports heroes include golfer Greg Norman and athlete Cathy Freeman.

4 _____

Australia has a lot of world-famous modern artists and writers, including Patrick White, winner of the Nobel Prize for Literature. Movie-making has become a major industry and pictures like _Mad Max_, starring Mel Gibson, and _Babe_ have appeared in movie theaters around the world. The television industry has produced popular soap operas like _Neighbors_.

5 _____

Australia's wildlife is unique because Australia is an island. There are plants and animals in Australia that exist nowhere else on earth. The most famous are kangaroos and koalas. These strange animals carry their babies in pouches. There are also many dangerous animals, including sea crocodiles, snakes, and great white sharks.

2 Match the definitions with a word or phrase from the text.

a variety of people of different origins (paragraph 1) a multi-cultural society

1 foreigners who come to live in a country (paragraph 1) _____

2 way of life and traditions (paragraph 2) _____

3 people who everyone likes and admires (paragraph 3) _____

4 a type of television series (paragraph 4) _____

5 animal life (paragraph 5) _____

3 Read the text again. Then, write answers.

1 What is Australia's second biggest city?
_____.

2 Who arrived in Australia two centuries ago?
_____.

3 What are the most popular Australian sports?
_____.

4 What cultural industries are important in Australia?
_____.

5 Why are there animals and plants that you can only find in Australia?
_____.

Vocabulary

Word formation: prefixes

1 Write the opposites. Use the prefixes *dis-*, *il-*, *im-*, *in-*, *ir-*, or *un-*.

kind   unkind

1 finite   _____
2 patient   _____
3 honest   _____
4 legal   _____
5 visible   _____
6 tidy   _____
7 obedient   _____
8 correct   _____
9 replaceable _____
10 possible _____
11 fortunate _____

2 Write labels for the pictures. Use adjectives from exercise 1.

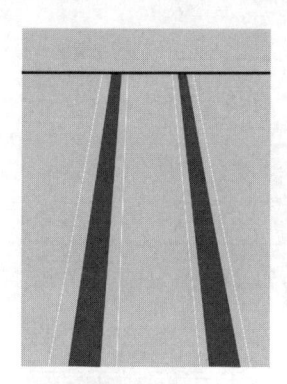

infinite    1 _____

2  _____   3 _____

4  _____   5 _____

3 Complete the definitions. Use the words in the box.

> ~~disobedient~~ illogical immobile
> immoral independent infinite
> invisible irresponsible unpleasant

Rover never does what I say. He's disobedient.

1 You can't see it. It's _____.
2 That doesn't make sense! It's _____.
3 She never asks for help. She's _____.
4 Time and space go on for ever. They're _____.
5 It never moves. It's _____.
6 It isn't very nice. It's _____.
7 Their small child plays in the road. They're _____.
8 They do some very bad things. They're _____.

6 Writing

Writing about vacations

1 Study Diana's model plan and notes. Then, write short answers.

MODEL PLAN AND NOTES	
Title: The worst vacation I ever had	
A Introduction: basic information	
when	last summer, August
where	camping, south coast of England
why	beach vacation
who with	my family
B Main part: *what, when, where, why,* etc.	
Sunday	all day on beach
Monday	rain all day, stay in tent, wet & cold in tent
Tuesday	am: rain again, feel sick 'cos bad cold
	pm: went home early
Wednesday & Thursday	all day in bed
C Conclusion: my opinions	
liked	Sunday
why	'cos all day on beach & hot & sunny
didn't like	other days
why not	'cos weather awful & camping in rain horrible
Go again?	Yes, I'd like to but not camp!

1 What is the title of Diana's composition?

   _____.

2 Where did Diana spend her vacation?

   _____.

3 Who did she go with? _____.

4 When did she go home? _____.

5 Why did she go home early?

   _____.

Planning and making notes

2 Complete Diana's composition. Use the notes in exercise 1 to help you.

The worst vacation I ever had was last summer in August. I went (1) _____.
It was (2) _____ vacation, and I went with (3) _____.
On Sunday, I spent all day (4) _____. On Monday, it (5) _____.
We (6) _____ and we were (7) _____.
On Tuesday morning, it (8) _____ and I (9) _____. In the afternoon, we (10) _____.
I spent (11) _____ in bed!
I enjoyed (12) _____ because (13) _____.
I did not like (14) _____ because (15) _____.
I would like (16) _____.

Your writing task

3 Write a composition. Use the notes you made in *Your writing task* on page 36 of the Student Book to help you.

Progress check

Units 5–6

Grammar

1 Rearrange the words to make sentences.

1 If / good, / to the park. / often go / the weather / I / is

_____

2 keep fit, / better. / I / If / feel / I

_____

3 I / my glasses, / can't read. / If / forget / I

_____

4 I / go to / If / some stamps, / need / I / the post office.

_____

2 Complete the sentences. Use the simple present or the future with *will*.

1 If we _____ (leave) now, we _____ (catch) the last bus.

2 I _____ (not go) to college if I _____ (fail) my tests.

3 If we _____ (not get) home soon, Mom _____ (be) very angry.

3 Which pairs of sentences have similar meanings (✓)? Which pairs of sentences have different meanings (✗)?

1 a) Carmen has to feed the cat.
   b) Carmen needs to feed the cat. ☐

2 a) Martine can't help at home.
   b) Martine doesn't have to help at home. ☐

3 a) We can't go to bed now.
   b) We don't need to go to bed now. ☐

Vocabulary

4 Complete the teacher's report. Use the words in the box and add prefixes.

| responsible obedient possible |
| kind tidy |

Adam leaves his things everywhere and his desk is very (1) _____ . He is also very (2) _____ and never does what the teachers say. He is (3) _____ because he says horrid things to other people. It is (4) _____ to teach him anything because he never listens. His parents are (5) _____ because they do not help him.

Communication

5 Complete the sentences. Use *have to* or *can't*.

1 You _____ stop.

2 You _____ drive fast.

3 You _____ leave your car here.

4 You _____ switch off your cell phone.

Units 5-6

Graded exercises

1 Complete the sentences. Use the first conditional.

(run fast / win the race)

If she runs fast, she'll win the race.

1 (eat all that / be sick)

If he _____,

he _____.

2 (not behave better / the teacher / get angry)

If she _____,

the teacher _____.

3 (go to Paris / visit the Eiffel Tower)

If she _____,

she _____.

4 (stay in the sun / be burnt)

If they _____,

they _____.

2 Study the chart. Then write four rules. Use *have to*, *don't have to*, or *can't*.

Rules	Basketball	Soccer
Run with the ball	✗	✓
Use hands	✓	✗
Kick the ball	✗	✓
Kick another player	✗	✗

Basketball players can't run with the ball.

Soccer players have to run with the ball.

Basketball players have to use their hands.

1 _____.

2 _____.

3 _____.

4 _____.

3 Write true sentences. Use *have to / need to*, *don't have to / don't need to*, or *can't*.

At school

I have to / need to be polite to the teachers.

I can't be noisy.

I don't have to / don't need to wear a uniform.

1 **At a rock concert**

_____.

_____.

2 **At the swimming pool**

_____.

_____.

3 **At home**

_____.

_____.

7 Champions.

1 Read the conversation. Then, correct these false sentences.

It's after the basketball final. Tom, Jet, and Meg are talking about Bud's injury.

Tom It was a great game. It's a pity Bud was injured.

Jet It can't be very serious. He wasn't taken to hospital.

Tom It hurt him a lot. It has to be quite serious. Luckily, it happened at the end of the game because Bud's the best player on the team.

Jet Yeah! He scored more points than anyone else.

Tom Here's Meg. Hi, Meg! How's Bud?

Meg I don't know. First, he was told by the referee that his leg was broken. Then they decided it wasn't serious. Finally, a cab was called and he was sent to the doctor's. Bella went with him.

Jet Did the *Lions'* captain speak to the referee about the player who pushed Bud?

Meg No. The referee said that it happened after the final whistle.

Jet That's not fair!

Tom Look! Here are Bella and Bud now. Bud's leg can't be broken. He's walking on it!

Bud was taken to hospital.

Bud wasn't taken to hospital.

1 Bud was injured at the **beginning** of the game.

_____.

2 First, Bud was told by **a doctor** that his leg was broken.

_____.

3 Then they decided it **was** serious.

_____.

4 Finally, he was sent **to hospital**.

_____.

Communication

Logical deductions: *must be, can't be.*

2 Complete the conversations. Use the phrases in the box.

> It must be.   ~~It can't be.~~
> Because it only has three wheels.
> It can't be.   ~~Because it's huge.~~
> Because it's called *Le Monde*.

A Is this his T-shirt?
B No, it can't be.
A Why?
B Because it's huge.

1 **A** Is this French?

B _____

A Why?

B _____

2 **A** Is this a fast car?

B _____

A Why?

B _____

33

Grammar

Passive

1 Which three sentences are passive (*P*)? Which three sentences are active (*A*)?

Many popular movies are produced in Hollywood. *P*

They show a lot of funny movies on TV. *A*

1 They teach children computer studies in school. __

2 The Euro is used in many European countries. __

3 They do not sell medicine in grocery stores. __

4 CDs are made at recording companies. __

5 You find elephants in Africa and Asia. __

6 Coffee is grown in South America. __

2 Change the active sentences in exercise 1 to simple present passive sentences and the passive sentences to active sentences.

A lot of funny movies are shown on TV.

1 _____.

2 _____.

3 _____.

4 _____.

5 _____.

6 _____.

Passive with *by* + agent

3 Change the sentences from active to simple present passive.

Most pop stars make videos.

Videos are made by most pop stars.

1 Millions of people watch soccer games.
_____.

2 The media create big movie stars.
_____.

3 TV companies send reporters to many countries.
_____.

4 Colleges interview new students.
_____.

5 Satellites send digital TV pictures.
_____.

6 The Japanese produce a lot of computers.
_____.

4. Complete the description. Use the simple present passive.

How a movie is made

First, a story is chosen (choose) by the movie producer and the characters' words (1) _____ (write). Then actors (2) _____ (audition) and (3) _____ (choose) by the movie director. Next, the team (4) _____ (send) to the filming location, and the different scenes (5) _____ (rehearse). After that, the scenes (6) _____ (film) several times by the camera operators. At the end of filming, the final material (7) _____ (choose) by the director. Then the music (8) _____ (add). Finally, the movie (9) _____ (show) in movie theaters around the world. If it is a good movie, it (10) _____ (see) by millions of people.

5. Write sentences. Use the simple past passive.

The first space shuttle (launch) in 1980.

The first space shuttle was launched in 1980.

1 Penicillin (discover) by Alexander Fleming.

   _____.

2 The Internet (use) by millions of people last year.

   _____.

3 *Yesterday* (sing) by the Beatles.

   _____.

4 *Guernica* (paint) by Picasso.

   _____.

5 *Jurassic Park* (direct) by Steven Spielberg.

   _____.

Logical deductions: *must be*, *can't be*

6. Write sentences about the pictures. Use *must be* and *can't be*.

He can't be hungry.

1 She _____ disappointed.

2 He _____ tired.

3 She _____ proud.

4 They _____ serious!

5 He _____ excited.

8 The secret of life.

1 Read the text. Then, choose and write the correct topic for each paragraph.

> Forever young   The human genome   The genome and medicine
> DNA testing and the law   Who is your dad?

DNA Testing

1 _____

1 Many scientists all over the world are studying the human genome. **This** is the complete genetic information needed to build a human being. **They** have not identified all our genes yet but they have already learnt a lot. One technique which is often used now is DNA testing.

2 _____

DNA testing is a way of identifying people from parts of the body, such as the hair. The police
5 already use it to help them identify dangerous criminals. **They** call this new technique "DNA fingerprinting". **It** will probably replace traditional fingerprinting in the future.

3 _____

Another use for this technique is paternity testing. **This** is the use of DNA testing to identify a child's real father. In the United States, paternity testing has become big business. Today, it is even possible to buy paternity-testing material on the Internet and do the test at home!

4 _____

10 Genetics is revolutionizing people's lives. In a few years time, scientists will be able to read each human being's personal DNA code. Doctors will be able to predict the illnesses a person might suffer from in the future and do something before **they** become sick. Genetics is also helping scientists to find new ways of saving people who suffer from terrible genetic illnesses.

5 _____

Last but not least, it is possible that scientists will soon identify the age genes. And if **they** do
15 that, we will all live for ever!

2 Read the text again. Then, write short answers.

What are many scientists studying?
The human genome.

1 Who uses DNA testing?

_____.

2 What do the police call DNA testing?

_____.

3 What technique can we use to identify a child's father?

_____.

4 Where can you buy paternity-testing material?

_____.

5 What will scientists be able to read in a few years time?

_____.

3 Find these words in the text. What do they refer to?

This (line 1) the human genome

1 They (line 2) _____
2 They (line 5) _____
3 It (line 6) _____
4 This (line 7) _____
5 they (line 12) _____
6 they (line 14) _____

Vocabulary

Word formation: suffixes

1 Complete the sentences. Add the correct suffix to each word.

> -ation   -ese   -ian   -ion   ~~-ish~~
> -ment   -ness

The Polish soccer team have won three games this season. (Pole)

1 He has a valuable _____ of ancient _____ coins. (collect, Egypt)

2 She is learning _____ at college. (Japan)

3 There are twenty-four hours of _____ in Norway in December. (dark)

4 My brother causes my parents a lot of _____ when he behaves badly. (embarrass)

5 I would like some _____ about train times, please. (inform)

2 Write the nouns. (Be careful! Sometimes there is a spelling change.)

organize   organization

1 express   _____
2 employ   _____
3 inform   _____
4 agree   _____
5 entertain   _____
6 happy   _____
7 kind   _____

3 Write the words in six lists. Add one more word to each list.

> actress   boxer   capitalism   communist
> soccer player   helpful   helpless
> hopeful   ~~sexism~~   socialist
> useless   waitress

1 abstract ideas   sexism   _____
2 people and ideas   _____ _____
3 female   _____ _____
4 occupations   _____ _____
5 being "without"   _____ _____
6 being "full of"   _____ _____

4 Complete the puzzle.

8

Writing

Writing about jobs

1 Study Natalie's plan and notes for the introduction of her composition. Then, write the abbreviations in full.

Title:	My drm job
Introduction:	info about me
job name	journalt
how long	for 2 yrs, since saw TV prog on journalm
why	'cos love travlg & meetg peop fm difft counts

	drm	dream
1	info	_____
2	journalt	_____
3	2 yrs	_____
4	TV prog	_____
5	journalm	_____
6	'cos	_____
7	travlg	_____
8	& meetg	_____
9	fm	_____
10	difft counts	_____

2 Write Natalie's introduction. Use the notes in exercise 1.

My dream job is to be a journalist. I have wanted to be a …

Expanding plans and notes

3 Here are Natalie's notes for the next two paragraphs of her composition. Complete the notes with the words and phrases in the box.

> away frm home a lot   Engl   interstg
> friendly   peop   ~~have to be 18+~~

Main part:	job requirements
phys	age: have to be 18+
	health: need to be fit
eductn	go to college, study journalm
langs	(1) _____ essential
personality	have to be confident, curious, (2) _____
	need to be interested (3) _____ & places
Conclusion:	advantages & disadvantages
advs	trav, meet peop, learn a lot
disadvs	long hours, (4) _____ , sometimes dangerous
my opinion	most (5) _____ job in world

Your writing task

4 Expand Natalie's plan and notes into full sentences and write two paragraphs.

To be a journalist, you have to be eighteen years old. You need to …

38

Units 7–8

Progress check

Grammar

1 Complete the paragraph. Use the simple present passive (*is / are* + past participle).

First, the tomatoes (1) _____ (grow) on farms. Then they (2) _____ (pick) by farm workers. Next, they (3) _____ (take) to stores and (4) _____ (sell). After that, the tomatoes (5) _____ (mix) with onions and spices and (6) _____ (put) on a pizza. Next, the pizza (7) _____ (cook) for ten minutes. Finally, the pizza (8) _____ (eat)!

2 Complete the sentences. Use the simple past passive (*was / were* + past participle).

1 Two paintings _____ from the house last night. (steal)

2 The burglary _____ at eight am this morning. (discover)

3 Fingerprints _____ on the window. (leave)

4 The neighbors _____ by the police. (question)

5 A man _____ near the house at 11pm. (see)

3 Complete the sentences. Use the simple present passive (*is / are* + past participle) or the simple past passive (*was / were* + past participle).

1 Every day, hundreds of e-mails _____ (receive) by the President.

2 English _____ (speak) millions of people around the world.

3 *Brave New World* _____ (write) by Aldous Huxley.

4 The *Star Wars* movies _____ (produced) by George Lucas.

Vocabulary

4 Write new words. Use the suffixes in the box.

| -ation | -ese | -ess | -ful | -ness |
| -ion | -ist | -ment | | |

1 disappoint _____   5 collect _____
2 kind _____   6 lion _____
3 inform _____   7 use _____
4 Japan _____   8 social _____

5 Complete the conversations. Use *No, it can't be.* or *Yes, it must be.*

1 A Is this your brother's notebook?

   B _____. It has his name on it.

2 A Is this orange juice?

   B _____. It's green.

3 A Is this your friend's jacket?

   B _____. He's wearing his jacket.

39

Units 7-8

Graded exercises

1 Write sentences. Use the simple present passive.

Hamburgers / sell / at *McBurger's*.
Hamburgers are sold at *McBurger's*.

1 Coffee / grow / in Brazil
   _____.

2 Movies / make / in Hollywood
   _____.

3 E-mail messages / send / on the Internet
   _____.

4 Pasta / eat / in Italy
   _____.

5 Baseball / play / in the USA
   _____.

2 Complete the newspaper article. Use the simple past passive.

Picture thieves hit again

A picture by Picasso was stolen (steal) from a London museum last night. The valuable picture (1) _____ (painted) by Picasso in the 1950s. It (2) _____ (buy) by the museum five years ago. This was the second Picasso picture to disappear from the museum in the last three years. The burglary (3) _____ (discover) by a cleaner. The police (4) _____ (call) immediately. All the museum workers (5) _____ (question). No fingerprints (6) _____ (find) in the museum. No other pictures (7) _____ (steal), nothing (8) _____ (break), and no noise (9) _____ (hear).

A van (10) _____ (see) outside the museum at midnight. The police think that both pictures (11) _____ (take) by the same thieves. A policeman said, "They must be smart because they didn't leave any clues."

3 Complete the sentences. Use *must be* or *can't be*.

She has done very well in her math test. (happy)
She must be happy!

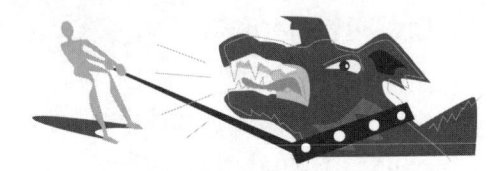

1 His dog looks dangerous. (safe)
   It _____.

2 They have run 20 miles. (tired)
   They _____.

3 The movie has been on for ten weeks. (boring)
   It _____!

4 He drinks a lot of water! (thirsty)
   He _____!

5 She's bought a new sports car. (rich)
   She _____!

40

9 In-line skating in the park.

1 Read the conversation. Then, write short answers.

Meg, Bella, and Jet are talking about their plans for the future.

Bella Is Tom joining us for lunch?
Meg No. He says he needs to find a job. He has to save money so he can go to college next year.
Bella Poor Tom! His mother said that she didn't want him to go. She thinks it's too expensive. What about you, Jet? Any news from drama school?
Jet No good news! But the bad news is that now my dad wants me to be a businessman! Yesterday he said he wanted me to go to business school.
Meg Amazing! Every day he wants you to do something different! So what did you say this time?
Jet I told him I hated business and I didn't like wearing a tie!
Bella Maybe tomorrow he'll suggest you become the next American president!
Jet I'd prefer that job to a businessman. You have to be a good actor!

Why isn't Tom joining them for lunch?
Because he has to find a job.

1 Why does Tom have to find a job?
   _____.

2 Tom's mother doesn't want him to go to college. Why not?
   _____.

3 Why does Jet's dad say he wants Jet to go to business school?
   _____.

4 Jet doesn't want to be a businessman. Why not?
   _____.

5 Why does Jet say he'd rather be the American president than a businessman?
   _____.

Communication

Reporting opinions

2 Write questions and answers.

your parents / think / learning Latin (useful)

What do your parents think about learning Latin?

They think it's useful.

1 most older people / say / pop music (rubbish)

   _____?
   _____.

2 your sister / think / in-line skating (great)

   _____?
   _____.

3 your friend / say / male cheerleaders (OK)

   _____?
   _____.

9

Grammar

Reported speech: with reporting verbs in the present

1 Complete the sentences. Use *say* or *says* and change the direct speech to reported speech.

I hate cleaning my room

Martine says she hates cleaning her room.

We're the best players on the team

1 Martine and Oscar _____.

I'm going shopping

2 Martine's mom _____.

I can't find my pet mouse

3 Oscar _____.

We don't like soccer

4 Oscar and his friend _____.

2 Read the conversation. Then, complete the paragraph. Change the direct speech to reported speech.

Martine I like the music! It's *Oasis*. They're my favorite band.
Oscar I don't like *Oasis* at all. They make a horrible noise. I like *Offspring* best.
Martine They're awful!

Martine says that she likes the music.

She says that (1) _____.

She also says (2) _____.

Oscar says (3) _____.

He says (4) _____.

He says (5) _____.

Martine says (6) _____.

42

Reported speech: with reporting verbs in the past

3 Complete the sentences. Change the direct speech to reported speech.

> I like steak and fries. It's my favorite food.

Oscar said he liked steak and fries.
He said it was his favorite food.

> I hate meat. I never eat it. I prefer vegetables.

1 Martine said _____.

   She said _____.

   She said _____.

> I enjoy eating traditional Italian food. Pasta is my favorite meal.

2 Martine's friend said _____
   _____.

   She said _____.

> I don't want to talk about food. I'm hungry and I want something to eat.

3 Oscar said _____
   _____.

   He said _____
   _____.

Indefinite pronouns

4 Complete the chart. Use the words in the box.

| ~~anyone~~ someone anything |
| something anything anyone |

	Affirmative sentences	Negative sentences	Questions
People	(1) _____	anyone	(2) _____
Things	(3) _____	(4) _____	(5) _____

5 Complete the sentences. Use *someone*, *something*, *anyone*, or *anything*.

Someone called to see you this morning.

1 We went shopping but we didn't buy _____.

2 She didn't meet _____ she knew so she came home.

3 I'm hungry. I want _____ to eat.

4 Did _____ call me this morning?

5 Listen! There's _____ upstairs!

10 The world of sports.

1 Read the text. Then, choose and write the correct topic for each paragraph.

An international sport   The origins of tennis   The big tournaments

Tennis – an ancient sport

1 _____

From its beginnings nearly one thousand years ago, tennis has grown into one of the most popular individual sports in the world. The earliest form of tennis was played by French monks in the eleventh century. They hit the ball against a wall with their hands and **they** called the game *paume*. The popularity of tennis increased and **it** spread to England and Italy in the fourteenth century. From the fifteenth century onwards, people played tennis with rackets on grass courts. It was in Britain that tennis developed into the sport we know today. But the name tennis probably comes from the French word *tenez* which means "take it".

2 _____

The first big tennis tournament was held at Wimbledon in 1877. In **that** year, there was only a men's tennis championship. The first women's championship was held at Wimbledon in 1886. In those days the players did not win a lot of money. Today, the most important international contests are the five Grand Slam tournaments. **These** are events which are held once a year in Australia, the United States, France, and Wimbledon in Britain. Only the best players compete in them and they win a lot of money.

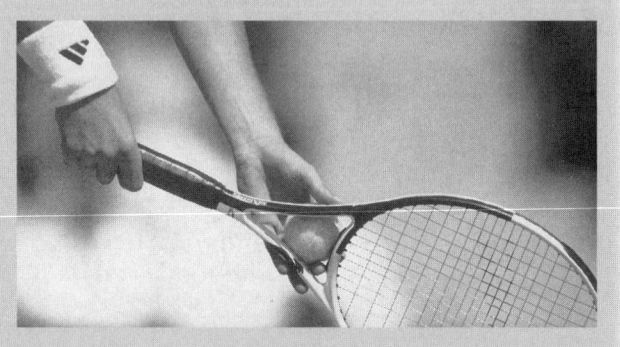

3 _____

Nowadays, tennis is an enormously popular international sport. The big Grand Slam tournaments are shown on satellite TV and **they** are watched by millions of people around the world.

2 Read the text again and correct the mistake in each sentence.

Tennis started in France **two** thousand years ago.

Tennis started in France *one* thousand years ago.

1 The earliest form of tennis was called *tenez*.

   _____.

2 Players started using rackets in the **fourteenth** century.

   _____.

3 The first big tennis tournament was held in **France** in 1877.

   _____.

4 The first **men's** tournament was held at Wimbledon in 1886.

   _____.

5 The Grand Slam tournaments are held **twice** a year.

   _____.

3 Find these words in the text. What do they refer to?

they called the game *paume*
the French monks

1 **it** (line 8) _____

2 **that** (line 16) _____

3 **These** (line 22) _____

4 **they** (line 29) _____

44

Vocabulary

New sports! Dangerous sports!

1 Complete the name of the sports.

k i c k-b o x i n g

1 a _ _ _ _ _ _ _ g
2 h _ _ g-g _ _ _ _ _ g
3 s _ _ _ _ _ _ _ _ _ _ g
4 s _ _ _ a-d _ _ _ _ g
5 b _ _ _ _ e j _ _ _ _ _ g
6 j _ t-s _ _ _ _ g
7 s _ y-d _ _ _ _ g
8 s _ _ _ -_ _ _ _ g

2 Write the sports names in three lists.

Air sports

hang-gliding

1 _____   2 _____

Water sports

3 _____   4 _____

Land sports

5 _____   6 _____
7 _____   8 _____

3 Complete the descriptions. Use the sports words from Exercise 1.

I went scuba-diving when I was on vacation in Belize. It was fantastic. I saw a lot of brightly colored fish.

1 I tried _____ in Chile at Christmas. It was great fun. At first, I fell down a lot in the snow. Then I had a class and I learnt to turn and stop.

2 We often go _____ because it's a good town sport. When I was learning, I fell over quite a lot but now I can jump on and off sidewalks.

3 The first time I went _____ I was very nervous. It took me five minutes to jump out of the plane.

4 My brother's joined a _____ club. My parents think it's dangerous. They say it is worse than boxing because you can kick the other person.

5 _____ is scary but it isn't a sport. You don't need to train or practice. You jump off a high bridge or a crane with a long elastic tied to your legs.

6 My favorite sport is _____ . It's dangerous and you have to understand a lot about winds. I jump off the top of a hill and sometimes I fly for over an hour.

7 I went _____ when I was on vacation in Spain. It's really good fun and anyone can do it. I love the feeling of going fast on water.

8 I do _____ when I go rock-climbing. It's great fun. You can run down a rock face!

10 Writing

Writing about special people

1 Choose and underline the correct connector.

I have seen a documentary about her *and / because* I have read her biography.

1 *Although / Because* she was British, she went to college in the United States.
2 After college, she got a job. *In addition / However*, she left her job and went to live in Australia.
3 She had a very rich way of life, *and / but* she knew a lot of famous people.
4 I admire her *although / because* she helped other people.

2 Read the introduction. Then, write short answers

The person I admire most

Introduction

The person I admire most is Gandhi, the famous Indian leader. Gandhi was a great religious leader. (1) *In addition / However*, he was a smart politician (2) *and / but* he led India to independence in 1947. Gandhi's original name was Mohandas Karamchand Gandhi (3) *but / because* after he died he became known as Mahatma Gandhi. Mahatma means "very great" and Hindus called him this (4) *although / because* they admired him very much.

1 Who is the person the writer admires the most?

    _____.

2 Where did he come from?

    _____.

3 What did Indian people call him after he died?

    _____.

Connecting ideas

4 Why did they give him this name?

    _____.

3 Choose and underline the correct connectors in the introduction.

4 Complete the main part. Use the connectors in the box.

> also ~~although~~ and because
> However   in addition   yet

Although Gandhi was Indian, he went to college and studied law in Britain. He returned to India and became a successful lawyer in Bombay. (1) _____ , he gave up his job in Bombay in 1893 (2) _____ went to work in South Africa. He returned to India in 1914 and became the leader of the Indian Nationalist Movement. Gandhi was an important person, (3) _____ he led a very simple life. (4) _____ , he lived with the poorest people in India. He organized disobedience movements, and he (5) _____ went on "hunger strikes". Gandhi fought the social injustice in Indian society (6) _____ he believed that everyone has the same rights.

5 Complete the conclusion. Use connectors.

Gandhi was killed in Delhi on January 30 1948, a year after Indian independence. He is the person I most admire (1) _____ he is an inspiration to leaders everywhere. He was a Hindu and an Indian (2) _____ he loved people of all religions and races. (3) _____ , he believed that rich and poor people all have the same rights.

Your writing task

6 Write a composition about a special person. Use connectors to link similar ideas or contrasting ideas.

Progress check

Units 9–10

Grammar

1 Complete the sentences. Use the simple past or the simple present.

1. He said that he _____ (not like) jazz.

2. She says her mom _____ (be) a great dancer.

3. They said that they _____ (like) snowboarding.

4. His friend says he _____ (work) in a garage.

2 Complete the sentences. Use reported speech.

1. Carmen: "I like Martine's dress."

   Carmen says _____.

2. Oscar and Martine: "We're going to the movies."

   Oscar and Martine said that _____.

3. Eddie: "My brother goes to college."

   Eddie says _____.

3 Complete the conversation. Use the indefinite pronouns in the box.

anyone anything nothing someone something

A (1) _____ has taken my bag!

B But there isn't (2) _____ here!

C Was there (3) _____ valuable in it?

B Look, there's (4) _____ on the floor.

A It's my bag! But there's (5) _____ in it!

Vocabulary

4 Find and circle seven sports words.

```
B U N G E K I C A B S E I N
A S N O B U N G U U N G F H
S C U Z O Q G D U S K I L A
B U N G E E J U M P I N G N
O B S E I J E T B P A C G G
A A B S E I L I N G K R I G
R D J E T S K I I N G I D L
D I V F S K Y D I V I N G I
R V I R K I C K B O X I N D
D I V I L I D I N G I I N I
S N O W B O A R D I N G Z N
T G R F K I C K B O X I N G
A B S E I D I N G E E T M V
S C U D I V B O A R H A N G
```

Communication

5 Complete the conversations. Use the answers in the box.

They think she's lovely. She says he's very kind. I think it's fantastic. He says it's hard work.

1. A What do you think about the new soap opera on Channel 1?

   B _____

2. A What do your parents think about your brother's new girlfriend?

   B _____

3. A What does she say about her new math teacher?

   B _____

4. A What does your friend say about his new job?

   B _____

47

Units 9-10
Graded exercises

1 Complete the sentences. Change the direct speech to reported speech.

I have a new scooter

Steve says he has a new scooter.

I'm going to London.

1 Barry says _____.

I hate hamburgers.

2 Molly says _____.

I'm learning to play the guitar.

3 Julie says _____.

I'm staying in bed all day!

4 Alex says _____.

I want to go to the movies

5 Mary says _____.

2 Rewrite the conversation in reported speech.

Stella There's a new math teacher at school.
Grace What's he like?
Stella He's tall and very good-looking, and all the girls in our class are in love with him!
Grace What's he like as a teacher?
Stella I don't know if he's a good teacher because I hate math! I never listen in class.
Grace Perhaps you'll work harder now!
Stella Well, I don't get bored any more. I sit and look at the teacher!

Stella said that there was a new math teacher at their school. Grace asked ...

3 Report a conversation you had with a friend or a member of your family.

My best friend / mom said ...

11 Graduation day.

1 Read the conversation. Then, put the events in the story (a–f) in the correct order (1–6).

It's the afternoon of Graduation day. Meg and Bud are at the airport, waiting for their flight.

Tom On behalf of all of us here today, I would like to thank you, Meg O'Connor, for your kindness, your beauty, and your lovely British accent. I would also …

Meg Stop it, Tom, please! Oh, I feel so sad. I don't want to leave you all.

Tom If I was rich, I'd come and see you in London. But that won't be for a long time, I'm afraid.

Meg If I had a lot of money, I'd take you all with me!

Bella Come on, you guys. Let's go. Bud and Meg have to get their plane.

Tom/Bella/Jet Bye, Meg! Bye, Bud! See you soon. Safe journey!

Jet Whose is this? It's a Lincoln High scarf. Is it yours, Bella?

Bella No, I left mine at home. It must be Meg's.

Jet You're right. It is hers. She's forgotten it.

Bella Well, we'll have to go to England now. To give it to her!

a Meg says she doesn't want to leave her friends. __
b Bud and Meg have to get their plane. __
c Tom says he'd go to Britain if he was rich. __
d Bella says they'll all have to go to England. __
e Tom gives a "thank you" speech. 1
f Jet finds a Lincoln High scarf. __

Communication

Well-wishing

2 Match the sentences (1–4) with the wishes (a–d).

1 I've broken my leg. b
2 I'm eighteen today. __
3 I've passed my driver's test. __
4 I'm flying to Spain. __

a) Well done!   c) Safe journey!
b) Get well soon!   d) Happy birthday!

Thanks!

3 Rearrange the words to make sentences.

to say / We / thank you / would like / to everyone / for coming here today.

We would like to say thank you to everyone for coming here today.

1 all the students, / we / On behalf of / to thank / the teachers / all their hard work. / for / wish

_____
_____

2 they / are grateful / have done / We / for everything / for us.

_____
_____

3 for everything / to thank / for us. / We wish / our drama teacher / she has done

_____
_____

4 for his help. / many thanks / Finally, / to our sports teacher

_____
_____

49

11

Grammar

Second conditional

1 Study the sentences. Then, complete the rules with the simple past or 'd / would.

If I had a lot of money, I'd leave school.

I'd go to college if I passed my tests.

If you got up earlier, you'd get to school on time.

1 We use _____ in the *if* clause.

2 We use _____ in the main clause.

2 Match the first parts of the sentences (1–2) with the second parts (a–e).

1 If I had more time, b

2 If I didn't buy so many clothes, __

3 If I studied harder, __

4 If I didn't go out so often, __

5 If I practiced more sports, __

a) I wouldn't do so badly in my tests.
b) I'd learn to play the guitar.
c) I'd be fitter.
d) I'd be able to buy a DVD player.
e) I wouldn't be so tired all the time.

3 Choose and underline the correct form of the verb.

If *I found / I'd find* a purse in the street, I'd take it to the police station.

1 If I had a million dollars, I'*d spend / spent* it all.

2 She *wouldn't / didn't* get wet if she wore a raincoat.

3 If Joe and I *rode / would ride* our bikes to school every day, we'd be fitter.

4 If he went out more often, *he'd find / he found* a girlfriend.

5 If I *had / 'd have* a scooter, I wouldn't get to school late.

6 If she didn't have a Saturday job, she *wouldn't have / didn't have* any money.

4 Write sentences. Use the second conditional.

If we (live) in the town center, I (not need) a motorcycle.

If we lived in the town center, I wouldn't need a motorcycle.

1 If I (sing) better, I (form) a rock band.

_____
_____.

2 If he (not eat) so many fries, he (feel) better.

_____
_____.

3 If she (go) to the gym twice a week, she (feel) much fitter.

_____
_____.

4 If you (clean) your room, your mom (not get) angry.

_____
_____.

5 If I (not play) basketball every Saturday morning, I (get) really bored.

_____
_____.

6 If they (listen) in class, they (understand) a lot more.

_____
_____.

5 Look at the picture and continue the chain. Use the second conditional.

(you lend me some money)

If you lent me some money, I'd buy a new guitar.

1 (I buy a new guitar)

If I bought a new guitar, _____ _____.

2 (I form a rock band) _____ _____.

3 (I become a star) _____ _____.

4 (I be very rich) _____ _____.

(I give your money back)

Possessive pronouns

6 Complete the chart.

Possessive adjectives	Possessive pronouns
my	mine
your	(1) _____
her	(2) _____
(3) _____	his
its	(4) _____
our	(5) _____
(6) _____	yours
their	(7) _____

7 Complete the sentences.

Are these Eddie's shoes? (Oscar)

No, they aren't *his*. They're *Oscar's*.

1 Is this your sister's book? (my brother)

No, it isn't _____.

It's _____.

2 Is that your parents' new car? (my grandpa)

No, it isn't _____.

It's _____.

3 Are those Martine's sunglasses? (Carmen)

No, they aren't _____.

They're _____.

4 Is that our pizza? (Carmen and Eddie)

No, it isn't _____.

It's _____.

12 Varieties of English.

1 Read the text. Then, choose and write the correct question (A–E) for each paragraph (1–4).

A Is English responsible for the disappearance of other languages?
B How many people speak English today?
C Will English break up into different languages?
D What are the "new Englishes"?
E Why has English become an international language?

Many types of English

1 _____

There has never been a language spoken by so many people in so many places as English. Today about 1.5 billion people speak English – that is nearly a quarter of the world's population. But it is the mother tongue for only 20 per cent of these people. For 1.1 billion people, English is a second or a foreign language.

2 _____

English has become the international language used in communications, business, and science. One reason for this is that English is spoken in one of the most powerful countries in the world, the USA. The American economy and culture, including its language, influence the modern world.

3 _____

Some people are afraid that their native languages will simply disappear if everyone speaks English. This would be a tragedy. A language carries the cultural identity of its speakers. It is a window to their unique view of the world. If a language dies, it is lost forever.

4 _____

Non-native speakers around the world have transformed and adapted English to their own special needs. There are now many different varieties of English, such as Indian, Caribbean, and pidgin English in parts of Africa. The dictionaries of these "new Englishes" contain words that no native speaker of standard English would recognize.

5 _____

Some people who study languages believe that these "new Englishes" are the origins of new languages. They predict that English will break up in a similar way to Latin, which produced a number of new languages, including Italian, Spanish, and French. It is also possible that a completely different language, such as Chinese or Spanish, will become the new universal language. But, right now, international English seems well established as the global language.

2 Are the sentences true or false?

About 1.1 billion people in the world speak English as their mother tongue.
False

1 Some people are afraid that English will disappear. _____

2 Native speakers around the world have transformed and adapted English to their own special needs. _____

3 It is possible that these "new Englishes" will develop into new languages. _____

4 Chinese and Spanish are the other two global languages. _____

3 Find words in the text with these meanings.

first language (line 5) mother tongue

1 global (line 8) _____

2 special (line 18) _____

3 changed (line 21) _____

4 types (line 23) _____

5 beginnings (line 28) _____

Vocabulary

Word families

1 Complete the chart.

Noun	Verb
actor	to act
(1) _____	arrive
help	(2) _____
origin	(3) _____
hope	(4) _____
(5) _____	argue
use	(6) _____
discussion	(7) _____
information	(8) _____

2 Complete the sentences. Use an adjective or an adverb.

My new grammar book is very heavy but it isn't very useful!

1 _____ , they checked the weather report and they didn't go out in the storm. (fortune)

2 She's very sick but the doctors are _____ that she will get better. (hope)

3 The Inuit people _____ lived in Northern Canada and Greenland. (origin)

4 She's very _____ that she'll get the job. (confidence)

5 Her mother gets angry because he isn't very _____ at home. (help)

3 Complete the sentences with some of the adjectives in the box. Then, complete the puzzle.

fortunate	happy	helpless	honest
~~hopeless~~	polite	possible	useless

1 They will never win a game. It's hopeless.

2 They're very _____ . They're both rich and healthy.

3 We were very _____ to see our grandparents.

4 Human babies are _____ for a very long time.

5 Your new boyfriend's always very _____ . I like him very much.

6 He isn't very _____ . He tells us things that aren't true.

7 It's _____ that a human will walk on Mars in the next fifty years.

8 This thing's _____ because it's broken. You can throw it away.

```
        ¹h
    ²   o
³       p
    ⁴   e
 ⁵      l
 ⁶      e
 ⁷      s
 ⁸      s
```

12

Writing

Writing about special occasions

1 Study Gavin's composition plan and notes. Then, write answers.

MODEL PLAN AND NOTES

Title: The best weekend of my life

A Introduction: basic information
where	Disneyland Paris, France
when	6 months ago
who with	my parents
how	flew to Paris, Friday October 26

B Main part: when, what, where, etc
Saturday morning	went Discoveryland & took trip to moon on space shuttle visited stars in space ship
11am	saw fantastic parade of Disney characts in Main Street
lunchtime	Pizzaburger at Buzz Pizza Palace
afternoon	went Frontierland, saw Indian camp & met Indian chief
5pm	had fantastic choc cookies, bought Mickey ears for brother in Disney store
6pm	watched Buffalo Bill Wild West Show

C Conclusion: going home, my opinion
Sunday am	visited Paris on tour bus
pm	flew home
my opinion	never forget that weekend

---

1 When did Gavin go to *Disneyland Paris*?
   _____.

2 What did he visit first?
   _____.

3 What did he see in Main Street USA?
   _____.

4 What did he do next?
   _____.

5 What did he do before the Buffalo Bill Show?
   _____.

Sequencing words

2 Complete Gavin's composition.

My name is Gavin and I live in Windsor, England. The best weekend of my life was six months ago. My parents took me

(1) _____.

We traveled (2) _____.

The next day was magical! First, we

(3) _____

and (4) _____

_____.

After that, we (5) _____

_____.

Then, for lunch (6) _____

_____!

Next, we (7)_____.

We saw (8) _____

and (9) _____.

At 5pm, I (10) _____.

Later, (11) _____.

Finally, (12) _____.

On Sunday, before we

(13) _____

we (14) _____.

I will never (15) _____.

Your writing task

3 Write a composition about one of these topics. Use dates, days, times, and sequencing words to describe the events. Use the composition in exercise 2 to help you.

A fantastic party
The best vacation of my life
The day I met my best friend

Progress check

Units 11–12

Grammar

1 Match the first parts of the sentences (1–4) with the second parts (a–d).

1 If we had a lot of money, __
2 If she worked harder, __
3 If they didn't go to the gym, __
4 If he invited me out, __

a) she'd get better test scores.
b) I'd say no.
c) we'd spend it all immediately!
d) they wouldn't be so fit.

2 Write sentences. Use the second conditional.

1 If he (get) really fit, he (go) snowboarding.
   _____

2 We (learn) more if we (work) harder.
   _____

3 If she (find) an evening job, she (save) some money.
   _____

4 If I (have) a dog, I (take) it everywhere with me.
   _____

3 Change the sentences. Use possessive pronouns.

It's my coffee.   It's mine.

1 They're his sneakers.   _____
2 It isn't their computer. _____
3 It's our car.   _____
4 They aren't her sunglasses. _____
5 It's your towel.   _____

Vocabulary

4 Complete the chart.

Noun	Adjective
confidence	(1) _____
(2) _____	fortunate
(3) _____	helpful
honesty	(4) _____
origin	(5) _____
(6) _____	polite
(7) _____	possible
use	(8) _____

Communication

5 Complete the conversations. Use the well-wishes in the box.

1 A I'm seventeen today.
  B _____.

2 A Bye. I'm getting the plane tonight.
  B _____!

3 A We've won the basketball cup!
  B _____.

4 A I have a bad cold.
  B _____.

Units 11–12

Graded exercises

1 Rearrange the words to make sentences.

If / a spider / he found / he'd scream. / in the shower,

If he found a spider in the shower, he'd scream.

1 If / a lot of money, / he'd buy / he had / a new car.

   If _____

2 If / I'd keep it. / some money in the street, / I found

   If _____

3 If / they wouldn't / have to walk. / a car, / they had

   If _____

4 If / the Internet a lot. / we had a computer, / we'd use

   If _____

2 Complete the conversation. Use *Whose* or the correct possessive pronoun.

Mandy What a mess! Come on, let's clear up.
Danny Whose are these Bob Marley CDs?

Are they (1) _____ , Mandy?

Mandy No, they aren't (2) _____ . I hate reggae. I think they're Jill's.
Danny You're right. They must be

(3) _____ . She's crazy about reggae.

Mandy (4) _____ is that black bag?

Danny Maybe it's Kathy's. Look, it is

(5) _____ . It has her name on it.

Mandy This looks like Billy's jacket.
Danny No, it isn't (6) _____ . He sold it

to me. It's (7) _____ now.

Mandy Wow! Look at these shoes! They're very big!
Danny And smelly! They must be Dave's.
Mandy They can't be (8) _____ . He was wearing his boots.
Danny Billy has big feet. They must be

(9) _____ .

Mandy Yeah, I think you're right.
Danny Listen! I can hear a car. I hope it isn't my parents' car.
Mandy Don't be silly! It can't be

(10) _____ . They're staying with some friends in Chicago.

Danny Oh, no! There's a black and white rat on the shelf. Someone's

forgotten it. (11) _____ is it?

Mandy I don't know and I don't care. Where's your cat?

3 Complete the sentences for you. Use the second conditional.

1 If I didn't have to go to school, _____

   _____.

2 I'd be proud if _____.

3 If I won a free vacation, _____

   _____.

4 If I had $10,000, _____.

6 I'd be scared if _____.

7 If I met Britney Spears, _____

   _____.

8 If I spoke English well, _____

   _____.